Living Values: An Educational Program
Educator Training Guide

Living Values:
An Educational Program
Educator Training Guide

DEVELOPED AND WRITTEN BY

Diane G. Tillman and Pilar Quera Colomina

WITH SPECIAL CONTRIBUTIONS FROM

Carol Gill

Neil Hawkes

Peter Williams

Health Communications, Inc.
Deerfield Beach, Florida

www.hci-online.com

Library of Congress Cataloging-in-Publication Data

Tillman, Diane
    Living Values, an Education Program : educator training guide / developed and written by
Diane G. Tillman and Pilar Quera Colomina with special contributions from Carol Gill,
Neil Hawkes, Peter Williams.
       p.   cm.
    Includes bibliographical references.
    ISBN 1-55874-883-0
    1. Moral education. 2. Living Values, an Educational Program. 3. Values—Study and teaching.
4. Teachers—Training of. I. Quera Colomina, Pilar. II. Title.

LC268.T554 2001
372'.01'1407—dc21

2001016666

ISBN 1-55874-883-0

Living Values: An Educational Program is a partnership among educators around the world. This program is supported by UNESCO and sponsored by the Spanish Committee of UNICEF, the Planet
Society, and the Brahma Kumaris, in consultation with the Educational Cluster of UNICEF (New York).

HCI, its Logos and Marks are trademarks of Health Communications, Inc.

Visit the Living Values Web site *www.livingvalues.net*

Publisher: Health Communications, Inc.
        3201 S.W. 15th Street
        Deerfield Beach, FL 33442-8190

Cover redesign and inside book design by Lawna Patterson Oldfield
Cover artwork by Frow Steeman
Original editors: Lynda Felder and Diane Holden

CONTENTS

CHAPTER III: HANDOUTS AND OVERHEAD MASTERS

**For use with
Training
Components**

Overhead Masters for Making Transparencies

ACKNOWLEDGMENTS

Thank you to educators around the world for your collaboration: Dominique Ache, France; Sue Emery, Greece; Maria Elisa Garcia de Jurado, Mexico; Sabine Levi, France; Monique Liger, France; Marcia Maria Lins de Medeiros, Brazil; Mila Ramgoolam, Mauritius; Enrique Simo, Spain; Radhika Sripati, India; and Vivien Von Son, Mexico.

Special thanks to Frow Steeman for the cover art work, David Warrick Jones for his technological support, and Carol Gill, Lynda Felder and Diane Holden for their loving willingness to proof and edit.

INTRODUCTION

Since its inception, training has been an integral part of *Living Values: An Educational Program*. This guide, the *LVEP Educator Training Guide,* brings together the experience of educators from different countries who conducted training seminars in twenty-one countries during the first phase of the program. The first train-the-trainer session took place in Oxford, England, July 1997.

As Living Values Education training took place around the world, trainers listened to different needs expressed. Some educators wanted to know more about values: What were they? How could they be taught? Others were concerned about deteriorating student behaviors. While teaching values was essential at this point in time, they felt the lack of attentiveness in students would undermine the attempt. In response to these issues, LVEP trainers developed the workshop sessions contained in this guide. This *Educator Training Guide* is designed to help trainers conduct LVEP educator trainings, which can be invaluable for teachers to establish a values-based atmosphere.

Within this book are workshop sessions for values awareness, creating a values-based atmosphere and skills for creating such an atmosphere. The sessions ask educators to look at their own values, the emotional needs of children, cooperative collaboration and communication in the classroom, building positive behaviors, and establishing values-based discipline. Sample training agendas are offered for one-, two-, and three-day educator training and a train-the-trainer (TTT) session. There are also introductory sessions, values activities groupings and process questions, and information about evaluation and adult presentation skills. We encourage you, as trainers, to first assess the needs of a particular group and site, and then tailor the training by selecting components that are a good match for those needs.

Some of the materials within this guide can be used to train Living Values Parent Group facilitators, and facilitators for Living Values Activities for Refugees and Children-Affected-by-War. However, these two types of training involve additional sessions not included in this guide.

Thank you for your interest in *Living Values: An Educational Program* and values education. We hope you find the workshops beneficial and your work with students even more rewarding.

Using the LVEP Educator Training Guide

The *LVEP Educator Training Guide* is organized in three main chapters, which are briefly described below. LVEP trainers will also need to work with the appropriate Living Values Activities Books.

Chapter I: Designing the Training

Describes the difference between TTTs (Train-the-Trainers) and ETs (Educator Training, Teacher Training). Discusses the aims of training, factors to consider when designing training, suggested qualifications of participants, the order and timings of the training components and sample training agendas.

Chapter II: Training Components

Steps through the content and process information for sessions within each training component. Since workshops build on each other, we suggest that you follow the order in which they are presented. Many topics include more than one session so that you can tailor the training to suit the time available and needs of the educators at any particular site.

Chapter III: Handouts and Overhead Masters

Provides participant handouts for several sessions as well as overhead masters that can be made into transparencies. Some handouts are useful for introducing this values education program to school personnel or Boards of Education. The overheads are available in color on the LVEP Web site, http://*www.livingvalues.net*.

CHAPTER I:

Designing the Training

DESIGNING THE TRAINING

Train the Trainer (TTT) or Educator Training?

The initial Living Values: An Educational Program TTT session started in the summer of 1997 in Oxford, England. Since that time they have bloomed around the globe. TTTs are often five- or six-day residential training.

The TTT is designed to train experienced educators and teacher trainers to conduct LVEP educator training sessions. We assume that TTT participants are already skilled in giving presentations and facilitating groups. At Oxford, the TTTs did include a review of adult presentation skills, but developing such skills is beyond the scope of the training. With only five or six days, we can effectively cover the basics of the program, its history and core assumptions, key concepts and processes and how to get the best use of the *Educator Training Guide.* It is recommended that trainees use the materials with students, and help with a training as a "coach" prior to attempting a training on their own.

The Educator Training is a seminar for educators working with children or young adults in their own classrooms. Most LVEP seminars are Educator

Trainings and not TTTs. Depending on the country or the preference of the trainer, the session can be called *LVEP Teacher Training, LVEP Educator Seminar* or *LVEP Educator Training*. Also, to take into account the time limits of participants, LVEP Educator Trainings can vary considerably. Most take from one to three days. We recommend at least two days to allow professionals the time to experience, as well as learn about, values-based education and the skills essential for creating that atmosphere in the classroom.

Description of an LVEP Training

During *Living Values: An Educational Program* trainings, educators participate in values awareness sessions. They are asked to reflect on their own values, offer their ideas on elements within a values-based atmosphere, and imagine an optimal classroom environment. After teachers discuss their ideas on the best teaching practices, LVEP's theoretical model and the rationale behind the variety of values activities is presented. This is followed by one or more sessions engaged in LVEP values activities for children and/or young adults. The workshop then turns to skills for creating a values-based environment. In longer trainings this includes: acknowledgement, encouragement, and positively building behaviors; active listening; conflict resolution; collaborative rule making; and values-based discipline.

Participant Qualifications and Current Status

Educator Trainings

LVEP Educator Training is for educators with an interest in values-based education. The values activities for children and the process for creating a values-based atmosphere is suitable for educators in primary and secondary schools, nursery schools and day-care centers. We have also done the activities with university students. The trainings are not restricted to professional educators with university degrees. Many adults who work with children have shown an interest and commitment to values awareness and the development of positive social skills. Individuals such as scout leaders and adult volunteers are leading the values activities quite successfully.

TTTs for Teacher Trainers

The audience for LVEP TTTs should be professional educators: teachers, teacher trainers, education officials and psychologists who already have existing skills in training adults or facilitating groups. Ideally, they will have already taken a short LVEP Educator seminar and used the values activities with children or young adults. They should aim to serve as LVEP teacher trainers and commit to conducting at least two LVEP educator training sessions in their own community or country.

Parent Facilitators

Those who want to conduct Living Values Parent Groups should be psychologists, parent educators or teachers with a background in psychology and facilitation skills.

Please note that by no means do we expect a participant in a one-day parent facilitator training session to instantly become a trainer. Our intent is to familiarize professionals with parent group experience with the Living Values Parent Group Process, and some additional parenting skills. After participants have facilitated several groups, they can share the process with other skilled parent group facilitators.

Designing the Training

TTTs can add an extra day or two at the end of the seminar for participants who wish to facilitate Living Values Parent Groups. You can find suggested training sessions for parent facilitators at the end of the sample TTT agenda. This is included as the sixth day of training after a five-day TTT. This training guide does not cover additional information about the parenting groups. The *Living Values Parent Groups: A Facilitator Guide* covers this topic in detail.

Facilitators for Values Activities for Refugees and Children-Affected-by-War

Please note that the LVEP Educator Training Guide does not cover all the sessions for becoming a "trainer" for LVEP's values program for refugees and children-affected-by-war. We strongly suggest that anyone who wants to be a trainer for LVEP's Living Values Activities for refugees and children-affected-by-war be a psychologist with a strong background in education, or a teacher with a strong background in psychology. Excellent group process skills are important. If there is a demand for this training in your country or region, please let your Living Values Regional Coordinator know. She or he will contact the LVEP International Office. Participants must be qualified.

Because of the unique situations in different countries, there may be a request to train teachers who are themselves refugees and live in refugee camps. The training takes at least ten days. They will then be able to use the program with their students. After a year of using the program, teachers with good presentation skills may undergo another ten-day training to learn to be trainers for the camps in the area.

Aims of the Training

Aims of an LVEP Educator Training

The aims are to:

- Become acquainted with *Living Values: An Educational Program* and a framework within which values-based learning can be implemented within a system.
- Explore skills to create a values-based atmosphere or ethos.
- Participate in an open and active process, exploring ways in which values can be expressed and modeled.
- Work with teams to experience the values activities for children.
- Network with other educators committed to positive self-development for children.
- Create enthusiasm for involvement with LVEP and values education.

Aims of an LVEP Train-the-Trainer

The aims of a TTT for participants would include the aims noted above, and also:

- Become familiar with selected components of the LVEP Educator Training Guide.
- Understand the importance of the trainer creating a values-based atmosphere of respect and love during the teaching and learning process of an LVEP Educator Training.

Selecting Training Components

Training Components are the building blocks of an LVEP training. The list below shows the Training Components in the recommended order of presentation. The detailed content of each training component is described in chapter II.

Suggested Order of Presentation

Training Components

1. Introductory Session
2. Values Awareness
3. Creating a Values-Based Atmosphere
4. LVEP Components
5. Values Activities with Educators
6. Skills to Create a Values-Based Atmosphere
7. The Process of Evaluation
8. Evaluation and Monitoring Forms
9. Using the Educator Training Guide (TTTs only)
10. Adult Presentation Skills (TTTs only)
11. Goals and Implementation Strategies
12. Closing Session

Depending on the length of the training, the number of Training Components, and the degree to which that component is explored, will vary. Most Training Components have only one session; but a few have two, three or four sessions. When there is more than one session, each session builds on previous sessions. Therefore, present the sessions within each Training Component sequentially. For example, for a two-day training, you might present the first session of Values Awareness. If the group wants a deeper experience in that area, either find time for more sessions or suggest a three-day training.

If the training period is short, the trainer needs to eliminate some Training Components. Keep in mind that, except for one-day training, it should be possible to include at least one session of every Training Component. (This excludes components listed for TTTs only.)

Use this guide in conjunction with *Living Values Activities for Children* and/or *Living Values Activities for Young Adults.*

Assess the Needs of the Group

It is important to assess the needs of the group. Is it a school site or school district? For an Educator Training for two schools, for example, you would want to talk with the principals/headmasters or the educator committee that handles the training arrangements. First make sure that they are familiar with LVEP and some of the values activities. Then review the Training Components and discuss the perceived needs at that site. If there are discipline concerns, they might want all four sessions of Skills to Create a Values-Based Atmosphere.

Training Components and Timing

1. Introductions	**Range of Time Required**

Welcome
Opening Remarks
History and Overview of LVEP
Sharing a Few Results
Introductory Activity
Aims/Agenda

1 to 3 hours depending
  on the length of the
  Opening Remarks and
  Introductory Activity

2. Values Awareness

Session 1: Our Values, Values
  Development in Children

1 to 1¼ hours

Session 2: Exploring Our Values
  as Teachers

1¼ hours

3. Creating a Values-Based Atmosphere

Session 1: Rekindling the Dream   1 to 1¼ hours
Session 2: A Tool Kit   1 to 1½ hours

4. LVEP Components

Session 1: Theoretical Model, Materials
  and the Variety of Values Activities

1 hour

5. Values Activities with Educators

First Series of Sessions: Doing LVEP
  Values Activities for Children and
  Young Adults

1½ to 5 hours

Next Session: Making It Practical–
  Processing the Experience, Sharing
  Ideas for Assemblies, etc.

½ to 2 hours

	Range of Time Required
An Exposition: Sharing Values Activities	½ to 2 hours

6. Skills to Create a Values-Based Atmosphere

Session 1: Acknowledgement, Encouragement and Positively Building Behaviors	¾ to 1 hour
Session 2: Active Listening	1 to 2 hours
Session 3: Transitioning to Values-Based Discipline	1 hour or more
Session 4: Conflict Resolution	1 to 1½ hours

7. The Process of Evaluation	½ to 1 hour
8. Evaluation and Monitoring Forms	¼ hour
9. Using the Educator Training Guide (TTTs only)	½ hour
10. Adult Presentation Skills (TTTs only)	1 to 2 hours
11. Goals and Implementation Strategies: A Blueprint	1 to 5 hours
12. Closing Session	½ to 2 hours

Timing (Hours)

The times shown are guidelines; set times to support the needs of your group and the training setting. If at a school, you will naturally assume the timing usually set aside for educator training at that site. Some schools may want you to start at 7:30 in the morning and others at 9:00. Some schools may want a one- or two-day training session and others may want you to do several short seminars after school. For residential training, you will have much more flexibility and may even want to arrange free time in the afternoon or visits to places of interest. The times shown in the Sample Training Agendas that follow suggest the amount of time to allow and the sequence for training components of different durations. Do not schedule training more than eight hours a day!

Sprinkle in a Few Values Activities

In the Introductory Session, you will find a few introductory activities that are games. You might want to include a couple of these or other values activities. For example, you might want to have the group sing a song at the end of the first or second session, or in residential training, assign them one of the Simplicity Activities, such as taking a walk and writing a poem. Think of a values activity that they would enjoy, and make it fun for everyone!

Sample Training Agenda, LVEP Educator Training

One-Day Agenda

8:00 A.M.–4:00 P.M.

8:00–9:15	Welcome and Opening Remarks History and Overview of LVEP Sharing a Few Results Short Introductory Activity Aims/Agenda
9:15–10:15	Values Awareness Session: Our Values, Values Development in Children
10:15–10:45	Break
10:45–11:30	Creating a Values-Based Atmosphere: Rekindling the Dream
11:30–12:00	LVEP Components
12:00–1:00	Lunch

2:00–3:20	Values Activities with Educators: Selected Activities on
	    Peace, including practicing conflict resolution skills
	    within the Peace Unit

3:20–3:40	Sharing Ideas for Assemblies and making it practical at their site
3:40–4:00	Questions and Answers, Planning Next Steps

Sample Training Agenda, LVEP Educator Training

Two-Day Agenda (Consecutive days)

Day 1:
8:00 A.M.–3:30 P.M.

8:00–9:30	Welcome and Opening Remarks
	History and Overview of LVEP
	Sharing a Few Results
	Introductory Activity
	Agenda
9:30–10:30	Values Awareness Session: Our Values, Values Development in Children
10:30–11:00	Break
11:00–12:00	Creating a Values-Based Atmosphere: Rekindling the Dream
12:00–1:00	Lunch
1:00–1:30	LVEP Components
1:30–2:15	Peace Values Activity: Conflict Resolution (with practice)
2:15–3:30	Values Activities with Educators—in small teams

Day 2:
8:00 A.M.–4:00 P.M.

8:00–8:15	Good morning. Begin with a song. Announcements.
8:15–9:30	Team Meetings of Values Activities continue
9:30–10:30	Skills to Create a Values-Based Atmosphere: Acknowledgement, Encouragement and Positively Building Behaviors Information About Active Listening
10:30–11:00	Break
11:00–12:00	A Little Active Listening Practice, then Transitioning to Values-Based Discipline
12:00–1:00	Lunch
1:00–1:45	Values Activities—Team Meetings continue • Processing the experience • How do we apply it in the classroom? • Sharing ideas for assemblies, etc.
1:45–2:00	Setting Up the Values Activities Exposition
2:00–2:30	Teams Share—An Exposition
2:30–3:00	The Process of Evaluation
3:00–3:30	Questions and Answers, Planning Next Steps

Sample Training Agenda, LVEP Educator Training

Three-Day Agenda (Consecutive days)

Day 1:
8:00 A.M.–3:30 P.M.

8:00–9:30	Welcome and Opening Remarks
	History and Overview of LVEP
	Sharing a Few Results
	Introductory Activity
	Agenda
9:30–10:30	Values Awareness Session: Our Values,
	Values Development in Children
10:30–11:00	Break
11:00–12:00	Values Awareness Session:
	Exploring Our Values as Teachers
12:00–1:00	Lunch
1:00–2:00	Creating a Values-Based Atmosphere:
	Rekindling the Dream
2:00–2:30	LVEP Components
2:30–3:30	Values Activities with Educators—in small teams

Day 2:
8:00 A.M.–3:30 P.M.

8:00–8:15	Good morning. Begin with a song. Announcements.
8:15–10:00	Values Activities for Children and/or Young Adults (in small groups)
10:00–10:30	Break
10:30–12:00	Skills to Create a Values-Based Atmosphere: Acknowledgement, Encouragement and Positively Building Behaviors Active Listening
12:00–1:00	Lunch
1:00–1:45	Communication: Active Listening practice
1:45–3:15	Transitioning to Values-Based Discipline • Rules and Expectations • Enjoying a New Quiet Signal • Time Out • Conflict Resolution
3:15–3:30	Sharing a couple of experiences, perhaps sing a song together or share a poem—or process questions and answers

Day 3:
8:00 A.M.–3:30 P.M.

8:00–8:10	Good morning. Announcements, housekeeping.
8:10–10:30	Team Meetings of Values Activities Continue—Conflict Resolution practice to be included in all small groups
10:30–11:00	Break
11:00–12:00	Making It Practical—Values Activities Team Meetings continue

- Processing the experience
- How do we apply it in the classroom?
- Sharing ideas for assemblies, etc.

12:00–1:00	Lunch
1:00–1:15	Setting up the Values Activities Exposition
1:15–2:30	Teams Share—An Exposition
2:30–3:00	The Process of Evaluation
3:00–3:20	Questions and Answers, Planning Next Steps
3:20–3:30	Sharing Experiences

Sample Training Agenda, LVEP Educator Training

Three-Day Agenda (One day a month for three months)

Day 1:
8:00 A.M.–4:00 P.M.

Use the LVEP Educator One-Day Agenda

Day 2:
8:00 A.M.–3:30 P.M.

8:00–8:40	Good morning. Share experiences doing the Values Activities during the last month.

• Successes
• Concerns and Needs

8:40–9:40 Skills to Create a Values-Based Atmosphere:
Revisit LVEP Theoretical Model
Acknowledgement, Encouragement and Positively Building Behaviors

9:40–10:10 Break

10:10–11:10 Active Listening

11:10–12:00 Transitioning to Values-Based Discipline
• Rules and Expectations
• Enjoying a New Quiet Signal
• Stopping the Cycle of Negativity

12:00–1:00 Lunch

1:00–2:30 Values Activities with Educators—Units on Respect and Cooperation

Designing the Training

2:30–3:00   Making It Practical: Team Meetings continue
- Processing the experience
- How do we apply it in the classroom?
- Sharing ideas for assemblies, etc.

3:00–3:30   Join as a large group again and share ideas for assemblies and decide on the next steps. Perhaps end with a couple of experiences, singing a song together, etc. You may want to have a question-and-answer session depending on the needs of the group.

Day 3:
8:00 A.M.–3:30 P.M.

8:00–8:45   Good morning. Share experiences of doing the Values Activities during the last month.
- Successes
- Concerns and Needs

8:45–9:45   Values Awareness Session: Exploring Our Values as Teachers

9:45–10:15   Break

10:15–11:45 A little more about Conflict Resolution—Practice Helping Students Understand Choices

11:45–12:45 Lunch

12:45–2:30	Values Activities with Educators—in Teams
	Units on Love, Responsibility, Simplicity
	Ask groups to decide on which values units they would like to focus.
2:30–3:00	The Process of Evaluation
3:00–3:20	Planning Next Steps
3:20–3:30	Sharing Experiences

Sample Training Agenda, LVEP Train-the-Trainer

Five-Day Agenda (Consecutive days)

Note:
- An optional extra day for Living Values Parent Group Facilitators is included at the end of this agenda.
- The following timing would be applicable to a residential TTT in a retreat-style setting. Adjust the timing if the TTT is held during the business/school day.

Day 1:
Evening
Session Only

5:30–7:30	Welcome
	Organizer(s) give short presentation(s) on Education and Values
	History and Overview of LVEP
	Introductory Activity
	Special VIP Presentations (or more time for introductions)

Day 2:

8:30–10:00	Aims and Agenda
	LVEP Results and Plans
	Values Awareness Session: Our Values, Values Development in Children
10:00–10:30	Coffee Break
10:30–12:15	Exploring Our Values: Creating Values Webs
	Creating a Values-Based Atmosphere: Rekindling the Dream
	Option: Assign a value activity during their free time, such as walking in nature and writing a poem to a tree.
12:15–4:00	Lunch and Free Time
4:00–5:00	LVEP Components
5:00–6:30	Values Activities with Educators—for Children and Young Adults. (The entire group divides into small groups for Ages 3–7, Ages 8–14, and Young Adults.)

Day 3:

8:30–10:30	Values Activities with Educators continue in small teams
10:30–11:00	Coffee Break
11:00–12:50	Skills to Create a Values-Based Atmosphere
	Acknowledgement, Encouragement and Positively Building Behaviors
	Active Listening

12:50–4:00   Lunch and Free Time

4:00–6:30   Skills to Create a Values-Based Atmosphere continue
              Transitioning to Values-Based Discipline
              Conflict Resolution

Day 4:

8:30–10:30   Participants teach Values Activities for Children and
              Young Adults in small groups

10:30–11:00   Coffee Break

11:00–11:30   The Process of Evaluation

11:30–12:30   Setting Up LVEP in Schools
              Questions and Answers

12:30–4:00   Lunch and Free Time

4:00–5:30   Small Team Meetings
              • Processing the experience of the values activities
                groups
              • How do we apply it in the classroom?
              • Sharing ideas, creating school assemblies, etc.

5:30–5:45   Teams set up Exposition

5:45–6:30   Exposition of Values Activities creations with all teams

Evening session   Sharing songs, skits and talents

Day 5:

8:30–9:30   Adult Presentation Skills

9:30–10:00   Using the Educator Training Guide

10:00–10:30   Coffee Break

10:30–12:50   Goals and Implementation Strategies
                    Small groups to meet in area/region teams to plan

12:50–2:00   Lunch

2:00–3:00   Planning teams share goals and implementation
                    strategies
                Last Questions and Answers

3:00–4:00   Sharing Experiences, Good-byes

TTT Option for Parent Values Group Facilitators

Day 5:   **Note to TTT Organizers: At the end of Day 5,
                do the following:**

8:30 P.M.   Overview of the *Living Values Parent Groups:
                A Facilitator Guide*

Day 6:

8:30–10:00   Session One: Participants pretend to be "parents"
                    taking part in the Process. Additional Facilitation
                    Skills.

10:00–10:30   Coffee Break

10:30–12:50   Session Two: Peace activities and the "Importance of
                    Play" Parenting Skill

12:50–2:00   Lunch

2:00–4:00   Session Three: Participants model another session.
                    Include Parenting Skill: Think Before You Say "No."

4:00–4:45   Questions and Answers, Dialogue

4:45–5:00   Sharing Experiences, Good-byes

CHAPTER II:

Training Components

1. INTRODUCTORY SESSION

Step One: Welcome

Welcome participants. If the training is hosted by a university, Department of Education, a school, or another organization, you can ask the leading representative(s) to open the session with a short talk or a few remarks about values-based education.

Step Two: Putting the Training in Context

The Need for Values-Based Education

It is always important to note the relevance of the training to the educators present. You might relate it to the current educational situation within the country, teacher needs or concerns or a current event important in that area.

The opening remarks listed below are possibilities. You can use them to stimulate your own thoughts, or relate them to one or two items that you think your group will find interesting.

Opening Remarks, Option A

UNESCO and the Delors Report, Learning: The Treasure Within

A small but growing number of educators around the globe and various governmental and nongovernmental organizations have been working on ways to introduce values-based education. This is in response to concern about our children, and the increase in all societies of violence, suicide, addiction and abuse. There is increased recognition that the missing dimension in educational systems around the world is the lack of focus on the affective domain.

UNESCO's recent Delors Report, *Learning: The Treasure Within*[1] cites the fundamental role of education in personal and social development and the necessity of building the awareness and ability to operate within the humanistic values we all share.

This report to UNESCO of the International Commission on Education for the Twenty-First Century by Jacques Delors and other leading educators served to invigorate a debate on the future of education. UNESCO strongly believes in education as a means of creating peace and international understanding.

A UNESCO conference in Australia in 1998 was organized around four pillars: Learning to Do, Learning to Know, Learning to Live Together and Learning to Be. While the first two are quite expected in the field of education, the latter two were not. They were explored as a result of the Commission's work and concern with the crises of social cohesion. People of the world must also "learn to be" and "learn to live together." Lifelong learning and the rekindling of the humanistic values was a focus for educators gathered from around the world.

---

1. Delors, Jacques, et al. *Learning: The Treasure Within*, Report to UNESCO of the International Commission on Education for the Twenty-First Century. UNESCO Publishing, 1996.

Training Components

In values-based education, the child is recognized as an individual, a whole person who functions as a complete being with other beings. Each aspect of personality is linked with another; the cognitive domain cannot be separated from the affective. *Living Values: An Educational Program* provides tools for educators to introduce a values-based educational approach.

Opening Remarks, Option B

Educators Are the Heroes

Around the globe the media blames educators for declining test scores and problems with today's youth. This negative view is such a contrast to the real picture. I see dedicated, hard-working educators, caring for students, striving to motivate and teach. I see teachers as those who continually respond to the needs of youth and the needs of the society.

Yet there has been a tremendous difference in the last twenty to thirty years in terms of overall student attitudes and behaviors. The difference is not in the determination, professionalism or caring of teachers. The difference is in the preparation of children who enter the school system and in the state of our society.

In recent years, two trends have especially increased the challenges of raising and educating children: growing materialism and violence in entertainment media. These have greatly impacted families, diverting time and focus away from traditional pastimes and the transmission of cultural and spiritual values. Many children spend far more time in front of the television than in front of their parents. Many adults spend less and less time enjoying and interacting with their children and families as they try to gain security and happiness through materialistic pursuits—or simply try to cope with a more complex world.

Training Components

Violence in entertainment has a profound influence on youth. Violent films, television programs and videos not only glamorize violence, they sanction inhumanity and normalize disrespect. As disrespectful words, gestures and expressions become commonplace, feelings of hurt, loneliness, alienation and anger in turn become more prevalent in children, young adults and even adults. As relationships deteriorate and divorce rates increase, many children have few adults in their life to nurture them.

In addition, watching more than four hours of television a day diminishes the development of children's psychomotor, language and social skills. The entry skills that the majority of these children bring to school are far below what they used to be.

Traditionally, values were transmitted by parents and communities. The call for values in education is asking educators to be the heroes—to fill society's void. It implores educators to be leaders in recognizing that technology and materialism are not enough.

As we begin the twenty-first century, we must tap into the creative energy and universal values that each human being holds within. Not only must we renew efforts to educate children, parents and ourselves, but also utilize our hopes and dreams for children to provide the emotional impetus. As educators we have the power to facilitate the development of universal values—and to reconnect with the values of our culture(s) and the universal values that unite us all.

Opening Remarks, Option C

The Spirit of the Living Values Initiative

Living Values: An Educational Program provides a means for educators around the world to collaborate—creating, sharing, and dialoguing as they introduce a whole series of values-based educational experiences. This cooperative partnership has produced positive results in a variety of educational settings. Each educator contributes in a unique way, yet each explores optimizing educational actions that have values at their core. Some of these ideas create situations of simultaneous teaching and learning where values become tools for building, integrating and sharing—where learning is both effective and an expression of what we believe in and what we live for. This program provides an important alternative that allows children and young adults to explore and understand values while immersed in their daily school experience.

In this process, it is vital to understand the underlying idea. There is the understanding that each human being has the potential for peaceful and loving attitudes and actions. When we as educators create open, flexible, creative, and yet orderly values-based environments, students will naturally move closer to understanding their own values and develop their own way of thinking. Children and young adults can perceive, understand, and act in a way that promotes peace and justice, and respects diversity. This program encourages a vision of a world free of exclusion, a vision of dignity and respect for each person and culture.

As *Living Values: An Educational Program* expands, it is even more clear that values are the key that allow us to comprehend, face and overcome challenges present in today's world. This program has provided many educators with a new feeling of the relevance of education—values-based educational activities are projects that are real preparation for life. In the past few years, educators around the world, educational communities, different educational organizations and NGOs (nongovernmental organizations) have participated wholeheartedly in the program. This cooperation creates hope for a better world and a just future.

Training Components

As teachers, we know that real values-based education is not something to be done once a week; it is at its best when integrated into the daily classroom experience. In any situation, a teacher can observe what is happening and reflect on the underlying values.

As educators, we can:

Generate learning experiences that create a space for students to reflect about their own values and the practical implications.

Create an atmosphere that enables the students to recognize the importance of values and their own responsibility in making positive personal and social decisions.

Opening Remarks, Option D

UN Convention on the Rights of the Child

The General Assembly of the United Nations on November 20, 1989, adopted the Convention on the Rights of the Child. The call for a values-based approach to education is inherent within each point of the Convention's Article 29.

Note: Article 29 can be found in chapter III. The trainer may wish to make it into an overhead transparency for the presentation.

Opening Remarks, Option E

Adding a Values Dimension to Howard Gardener's Multiple Intelligences Model

Trainer's Note: Peter Williams, a headteacher from the United Kingdom, finds that "left-brain" thinkers relate to values very easily when the following model is presented. Overhead masters are available in chapter III.

We are each a unique and valued person, with our own special part to play in shaping our own world and the world around us. Each of us learns and shows our talents in many different ways according to the effort we make and the opportunities that meet us every day. Recognizing and valuing the unique contribution of each and every person helps to further the human qualities and learning potential of everyone.

One of many useful models to help identify human qualities and human potential is Howard Gardener's Multiple Intelligences. The model suggests that there are eight interrelated dimensions of learning that help identify skills, abilities and behaviors in us all. They are:

- The Body/Kinesthetic dimension, as related to physical movement and sport.
- The Environmental/Ethical dimension, as related to our relationship with and caring for the living environment.
- The Logical/Mathematical dimension, as related to logical and abstract reasoning skills.
- The Musical/Rhythmic dimension, as related to sound and tonal patterns.
- The Interpersonal dimension, as related to person-to-person relationships and communication.
- The Intrapersonal dimension, as related to self-reflection, how we think and awareness of spiritual realities.
- The Verbal/Linguistic dimension, as related to the written and spoken word.
- The Visual/Spatial dimension, as related to sight, artistic endeavors and mental imagery.

Adapting this model, placing the Intrapersonal dimension, at the hub of a wheel, with the seven equally important dimensions forming the spokes of the wheel, helps to make sense of how we can each learn and apply our knowledge in different ways.

Training Components

The Significance of the Intrapersonal Dimension

Placing the Intrapersonal Dimension at the hub of the wheel underpins the understanding that:

1. All actions emanate from ourselves, whether bodily, environmental, logical, musical, interpersonal, verbal or visual.
2. We all have the capacity to develop in each of the dimensions to varying degrees of success, according to effort and opportunity.
3. All learning, thinking and actions begin with a thought in ourselves and are owned by ourselves.
4. Time to be still within ourselves, to churn over ideas and reflect, is just as important as being practically active.
5. The love of learning, love of one's subject, the pursuit of happiness and the love of humanity begins within ourselves.
6. The door to new eras of opportunity and future possibilities hinges on understanding ourselves.
7. At the heart of all learning is the capacity to understand and develop our core qualities so that we can relate to one another with decency, honesty, mutual respect, responsibility and tolerance.

The model offers the opportunity for each individual to develop according to his or her own capacity, effort and preferred learning style, where all dimensions and avenues of knowledge are given equal value and equal weighting on all spokes as well as the hub.

It is a model that welcomes:

1. The brain's logical and linear learning and individual effort as much as creativity, imagination, ideas and holistic learning.

2. An acknowledgment and appreciation of the subjective well-being of the individual as much as objective measurements.

3. The value of affective learning within individuals as much as cognitive learning.

It is often assumed that our talent develops exponentially. This is not so. We all arrive at points in our experience in which we do not know the answer or what to do next. We sometimes say, "We'll sleep on it," or meditate or reflect on what has been achieved before proceeding further. These inner reflections, thoughts and altered states of consciousness are at the heart of the development of our own intrapersonal dimension.

As the person recognizes and develops his or her unique qualities and spirituality, so, too, will the knowledge at the very center of one's own intrapersonal wheel intensify. It will then radiate into an ever-shining, living example of how to unlock and fulfill one's potential through thought, word, skill and talent.

Living Values: An Educational Program opens the door of understanding and offers personal strategies for action in the interpersonal dimension of learning.

Step Three: History and Overview of LVEP

Trainer's Note: In chapter III there are ten overhead masters on the history and overview of LVEP that you may wish to make into transparencies for your presentation. While the main points of information to be presented are on the overheads, listed below is some additional information.

Overhead 1: Exploring and Developing Universal Values for a Better World.

Living Values: An Educational Program is a values education program. It offers a variety of experiential values activities and practical methodologies to explore and develop twelve key personal and social values—twelve universal values: Peace, Respect, Love, Happiness, Freedom, Responsibility, Honesty, Humility, Tolerance, Simplicity, Cooperation and Unity.

Overhead 2: Living Values: An Educational Program Is a Partnership Among Educators Around the World.

This program is supported by UNESCO, sponsored by the Spanish National Committee of UNICEF, the Planet Society, and the Brahma Kumaris, in consultation with the Education Cluster of UNICEF (New York).

Overhead 3: Purpose

The purpose is to provide guiding principles and tools for the development of the whole person, recognizing that the individual is comprised of physical, intellectual, emotional and spiritual dimensions.

Overhead 4: Aims

The Aims Are:

- To help individuals think about and reflect on different values and the practical implications of expressing them in relation to themselves, others, the community and the world at large.
- To deepen understanding, motivation and responsibility with regard to making positive personal and social choices.
- To inspire individuals to choose their own personal, social, moral and spiritual values, and be aware of practical methods for developing and deepening them.

To encourage educators and caregivers to look at education as providing students with a philosophy of living, thereby facilitating their overall growth, development and choices so they may integrate themselves into the community with self-respect, confidence and purpose.

Overhead 5: Sharing Our Values for a Better World

Sharing Our Values for a Better World was the name of an international project begun in 1995 by the Brahma Kumaris to celebrate the 50th anniversary of the United Nations. This project focused on universal values. The theme—adopted from a tenet in the preamble of the United Nations' Charter—was "To reaffirm faith in fundamental human rights, in the dignity and worth of the human person. . . ."

Overhead 6: "Its Birth"

Living Values: A Guidebook was created as part of the international project, Sharing Our Values for a Better World. The guidebook provided value statements on twelve core values, offered an individual perspective for creating and sustaining positive change, and included sections on facilitated group workshops and activities. One section contained values activities for students in the classroom. That small chapter on classroom curriculum became the inspiration and impetus for this values education program when it was shown to Cyril Dalais, a Senior Advisor with UNICEF's Early Childhood Development Program in New York.

Living Values: An Education Initiative (LVEI) was born when twenty educators from around the world gathered at UNICEF headquarters in New York City in August 1996 to discuss the needs of children, their experiences of working with values and how educators can integrate values to better prepare students for lifelong learning. Using *Living Values: A Guidebook* and the

"Convention on the Rights of the Child" as a framework, these twenty educators from five continents identified and agreed upon the purpose and aims of values-based education worldwide—in both developed and developing countries.

Overhead 7: Living Values Educators' Kit (optional)

As a result of that 1996 meeting at UNICEF headquarters, the *Living Values Educators' Kit* was ready for piloting in February 1997. It began to be distributed and has been gaining momentum since!

The kit contains twelve sections:

1. Setting the Context
2. Commitment
3. Educators' Manual
4. Blueprint: Values-Based Curriculum
5. Values Activities for Children 2–7
6. Values Activities for Children 8–14
7. Values Activities for Young Adults
8. Parents/Caregivers Module
9. Appendix for Values Activities
10. Evaluations
11. Train the Trainers
12. Refugees Module

Overhead 8: Six LVEP Books

The content of the original *Living Values Educators' Kit* was expanded and separated into six books in 1999 and the early part of 2000.

Trainer's Note: If you wish to give more information about the books, refer to Training Component 4, LVEP Components.

- Living Values Activities for Children Ages 3–7
- Living Values Activities for Children Ages 8–14
- Living Values Activities for Young Adults
- LVEP Educator Training Guide
- Living Values Parent Groups: A Facilitator Guide
- Living Values Activities for Refugees and Children-Affected-by-War

Overhead 9: Where We Are Now

As of April 2000, over eighteen hundred sites in sixty-four countries are using LVEP. Educators indicate that students are responsive to the values activities and show interest in discussing and applying values. Teachers note that students appear more confident, are more respectful to others and exhibit an increase in positive and cooperative personal and social skills.

There are TTT sessions for different regions, as well as the annual Oxford TTT to which educators around the world are invited. At the TTTs, educators become LVEP trainers for other educators, and facilitators are trained to do Living Values Parent Groups. LVEP Educator Trainings are conducted in many regions and countries. Training is offered to countries with refugee camps in order to train educators to use the Living Values Activities for Refugees and Children-Affected-by-War.

The six LVEP books are currently available in English. Translation is ongoing in Arabic, Chinese, German, Greek, Hebrew, Hindu, Hungarian, Italian, Japanese, Malay, Polish, Portuguese, Russian, Spanish, Thai, Turkish and Vietnamese.

Overhead 10: Taking Place in Sixty-Four Countries

LVEP materials are being used at sites in sixty-four countries.

Additional Information About Partners

Trainer's Note: If you need additional information about organizations involved, the following is provided as a resource.

UNICEF

The United Nations Education Fund for Children is mandated by the United Nations General Assembly to work for the protection of children's rights, to help meet their basic needs and to expand their opportunities to reach their full potential. UNICEF mobilizes political will and material resources to help countries, particularly developing countries, ensure a "first call for children" and to build their capacity to form appropriate policies and deliver services to children and their families. It is a nonpartisan organization, and its cooperation is free of discrimination. In everything it does, the most disadvantaged children and the countries in greatest need have priority. UNICEF aims, through its country programs, to promote the equal rights of women and girls and to support their full participation in the political, social and economic development of their communities.

Brahma Kumaris: Spotlight on Values Education

For the past sixty-three years the Brahma Kumaris have been researching and teaching an understanding of the self that affirms the spiritual identity and the inherent goodness and worth of the human being. This learning experience uses the principles of silent reflection and contemplation to explore human potential and to help build capacity. As a result of this learning experience, there can be an effective change of awareness, attitude and values, and then behavior and way of life. The foundation for an improvement in the quality of life is a change in the understanding that we have of ourselves—in the perception of our inner nature, or being, and its impact on our surroundings. It is spiritual discipline that can generate the willpower to translate vision into action, principle into practice and rhetoric into reality.

The Brahma Kumaris have coordinated international outreach projects specifically dedicated to values as they apply to people's lifestyles. Projects dedicated to the United Nations, such as The Million Minutes of Peace Appeal (dedicated to the International Year of Peace), Global Cooperation for a Better World (a Peace Messenger Initiative), and Sharing Our Values for a Better World (in honor of the UN fiftieth anniversary), show that a better world will only come about through personal commitment and collective change.

The Brahma Kumaris, in their affiliation with UNICEF, place great importance on the holistic development of the child. The world conference on "Education for All"—held in Jomtein, Thailand in March 1990—served as a catalyst for education to take center stage as we move into the twenty-first century. The experts focused not only on universal access to education, but also on the quality of the content—what individuals are taught—the knowledge, values, principles and skills that give meaning and purpose to life and quality of lifestyles. *Living Values: An Educational Program* responds to the challenge set forth in Jomtien.

The Brahma Kumaris University is a nongovernmental organization in general consultative status with the Economic and Social Council of the United Nations, and in consultative status with UNICEF. An organization largely administered by women, the Brahma Kumaris pursue the goal of upholding the human rights of all people worldwide by calling into focus the worth of the individual, and the dignity and integrity of the human family.

Share a Few Results

Trainer's Note: There is an information piece with anecdotal results in Chapter III. Or, you can obtain current information on the LVEP Web site at *www.livingvalues.net.* However, if there are educators in your area who have been using LVEP, ask one, two or three of them to share their most rewarding moments.

Step Four: Introductory Activities

Trainer's Note: There are endless varieties of introductory activities. Please choose one that is appropriate for your setting and number of participants. If you have more than thirty participants, you may wish to consider playing a game rather than having individual participant introductions. The individual introductions could take place in smaller group sessions later in the training. In a setting where all participants know one another, you may wish to skip this component or have every person share one sentence. (See the following for a variety of options.)

Participant Introductions

Ask each person to introduce her or himself, giving their name and one sentence about a relevant topic. They could, for example, say why they are interested in values development, or name two values they would like to see in our society or the world.

For another example, have each person say who they are, where they teach, or why they are here.

"If I Were an Animal, I Would Be a . . ."

In this introductory activity, participants are to think of one of their favorite animals and the value or quality of that animal most important to them. Give each participant a sheet of blank paper with a straight pin at the top. Ask them to write the name of the animal (in big letters) on the top half of the paper and the value or quality of the animal on the bottom half. Explain that each person will be pinning her or his sheet of paper on the back of someone else, not letting that person see what is written.

In this introductory game, each participant introduces him or herself to another person and then asks one question. The first task is to figure out the type of animal written on the paper pinned on their back. The one question must be able to be answered by a "yes" or "no." For example, "Does this animal have four legs?" "Is it a mammal?" Once they figure out the name of the animal, they are to try and figure out the virtue or quality.

Once the participants understand the directions, ask them to pin their sheet of paper on the back of someone else, not letting that person see what is written. Play some music as the game begins. Allow it to continue for about fifteen minutes or until the noise begins to subside as people figure out the words on their back.

Variations: "If I were a flower I would be . . ." or have participants put the names of famous champions of peace or justice, or their heroes or heroines, and the quality they admire in that person. Or, ask each participant to write their favorite value at the top of a page, with a symbol representing it below. Then play the same game as above.

Icebreaker Bingo

Give participants a copy of the Icebreaker Bingo Sheet (from Chapter III) and ask them to circulate it, finding one person at a time who can sign one of the squares on the Bingo Sheet. If you have a large group, instruct people to fill in all the squares with names in order to win. If it is a smaller group, participants can win by having a straight line across any five squares. They can shout VALUES to stop the game and receive a token "prize." When you are sure everyone understands, start the game. Play background music while the game is in progress.

You may wish to change the content of some of the squares in the Bingo Sheet to suit your own "climate"—it can also be adapted for specific professions or cultures.

Dialogue with a Partner

Ask the participants to share with a partner their responses to the following questions. Allow about six minutes.

- With what animal do you identify? Why?
- What expectations do you have of the course?
- Why are you here?

Afterwards ask them to share their expectations. Note their comments on a flipchart then comment on how the themes of the course are (or are not) related to their expectations.

Past, Present and Future Values

This introductory activity takes about twenty-five minutes and works well with groups. It has been done very successfully with groups of 300 people, including an audience of children and adults.

Play music as you begin with the instructions. Give participants each a blank piece of paper. Say, "I would like you to reflect on a time when you were little. Think about how you looked and felt, what you played, the expressions on your face and eyes, and what values or qualities were important to you." (Give them a couple of minutes.)

As the music continues, say, "Write one, two or three of those values at the bottom of the paper you were given." (pause). When they are ready say, "Now think about yourself in the present. Picture yourself from the outside, and then how you feel on the inside. What do you care about deeply?" (Give them several minutes.)

"Write one, two or three of those values in the middle of the piece of paper." (pause).

When they are ready, say, "Now think about yourself in the future. What values do you want to have? What values will motivate you?" (Give them several minutes.)

"Write one, two or three of those values at the top of your paper. Fold the paper in three parts and tear it into three pieces. Hold your three pieces of paper in front of you, with the piece with your values as a child on the bottom, those of the present in the middle and those of the future at the top.

Stand and walk in silence around the room. You are presenting yourself in a different form. Experience the values you have written." (Give them two minutes to walk around the room.)

"Continue to walk slowly in silence as you return to your seats. On your way, give three different people your three pieces of paper, accepting one of their pieces in exchange for yours." Ask:

- "What was your experience?" Record the answers they call out on a flipchart. Write in one column the experiences and values that have to do with the "self" and others that have to do with "others." If the group gives you ideas that relate to education, write those responses under the word "Classroom."
- "How do the values on the pieces of paper you now have compare with the values you wrote down?" Record their answers on the flipchart.

—Contributed by Vivien Von Son

Step Five: Presenting the Agenda and Ground Rules

Trainer's Note: Ensure that participants have copies of the agenda. Briefly review the agenda, and ask for any questions.

Ask the participants what ground rules they would like for this seminar, modeling the collaborative rule-making skill under "Skills to Create a Values-Based Atmosphere." One rule you may want to share that you want, and ask the group to agree to, is starting each session on time. Promise that you will end on time.

Sample Ground Rules are below, supplied by Carol Gill. Produce your own with the group. One or two rules are fine.

Sample Ground Rules

- Start and end on time.
- Listen actively. Listen from the heart.
- Be brief. No "soap boxes."
- Build on each other's ideas.
- No idea is a bad idea.
- Leave "baggage" outside.
- No downward spirals.
- Create a network.
- Make magic happen.
- Have fun!

2. VALUES AWARENESS

Session One: Our Values, Values Development in Children

Facilitator's Note: A script follows, as some trainers have requested the thorough detail found in this type of format. Please feel free to adapt it to your own personal style.

Opening Remark

"Values affect our lives every moment. They are a guiding force in all we do and pursue. When our values are in congruence with our actions, we are in harmony. But what are values? And how did we develop them? I would like you to reflect on some of your values as I ask you to think about several things. Please write down your responses."

Process

Play some relaxing music, and begin the following *Reflective* exercise. Allow enough time for responses. Approximate pausing times are suggested, but each group is different. Observe when they are finished. Say:

- "I would like you to think of a person who has influenced your life in a positive way." (Pause for a few moments.)
- "What values or qualities did you see in that person that made a difference for you? Please write down the qualities or values that made it important to you." (Pause for a minute.)
- "If everyone in the world had that quality, or demonstrated that value constantly, would the world be different?" (pause).
- "I would like you to think of the songs you love. What values are reflected through those words and music? Write those down." (Allow two or three minutes.)
- "Think of poems, quotes and books that are important to you. What qualities are within them?" (Allow three or more minutes.)
- "What images are important to you? Think of your favorite scenes, views or perhaps statues. What values and feelings are elicited by those?" (Allow three or more minutes.)
- "Remember a few especially positive moments of your life—what feelings did you experience then? What value did you demonstrate in those moments?" (Allow four or more minutes.)
- "What values influenced your decision to become an educator? Write those down." (Allow three minutes.)
- "Think of what you enjoy most about teaching. What is it that you value within the moments you are remembering?" (Allow three minutes.)
- "What are values?"

Ask the educators to form groups of four within the room. Instruct them to introduce themselves and share some of their experiences and values from this exercise. While you may wish them to share for fifteen minutes, observe to see when most of the groups are finished. Some finish in ten minutes and others want twenty-five!

Training Components

When you have gathered the large group back together, say:

- "Now I would like you to take a few minutes to think about six values that are most important in your life. Please write them down." *(Play reflective music softly.)*

Ask participants to share and write their responses on the flipchart.

Then ask them to share the definition of values they wrote earlier. In past trainings, participants have generated some beautiful definitions.

You (the trainer) may want to share your thoughts about what values are.

Another thought you may choose to share is: Values and virtues are on the same continuum. We use a value as a virtue when we experience and treat people in our life with that quality. It becomes a value when we treat everyone with that quality, and use it to make positive decisions in our life.

Say, "A very interesting project was done several years ago called Global Cooperation for a Better World. In this project, thousands of small groups of people from all different cultures, religions, ages and socioeconomic statuses gathered in 129 countries to visualize a better world. They were asked to visualize how they would feel in a better world, how their relationships would be and what the environment would look like. Can you guess their responses?" Ask:

- "How would you like to feel inside?
- "How would you like your relationships to be?
- "What would you like the environment to be like?"

"It seems that not only do we want the same qualities in our relationships, but that human beings in all cultures share universal values. While we share universal values, we are not living the values we share. It is the premise of this program that if we did live our values, we would create a better world."

Content

Say, "LVEP is built on three core assumptions." (Overhead available in Chapter III.) "The first assumption is drawn from a tenet in the preamble of the United Nations charter, 'To reaffirm faith in fundamental human rights, in the dignity and worth of the human person. . . .'

1. Universal values teach respect and dignity for each and every person. Learning to enjoy those values promotes well-being for individuals and the larger society.
2. Each student does care about values and has the capacity to positively create and learn when provided with opportunities.
3. Students thrive in a values-based atmosphere in a positive, safe environment of mutual respect and care—where students are regarded as capable of learning to make socially conscious choices.

"It has been said that children form their values by the age of five. Adults are said to only change their values if they have a life-altering experience.

"It is true that children have strong tendencies in their personality at the age of five. It is said that values are caught, not taught. Many children have less than optimal home environments. Some have been harmed by watching abusive adult relationships, or been subjected to mistreatment themselves. I do not think that they want to carry with them negative personality patterns. While they are deeply affected and may at times act as though they do not connect with positive values, I do not believe that this is the case. It is my experience that all children like peace, love and respect—and would choose those experiences if they could."

Share one of your personal experiences, telling a story of a child who was able to change in a nurturing environment, or ask the audience if any of them would like to share a story of a child with initial negative behavior who changed in a nurturing educational environment.

Say, "Let's explore for a few minutes how you developed your values. I would like you to think back to a time when you were little, and remember those experiences when you learned what was important to you." (Play some music and allow them to reflect for a couple of minutes.)

- "Now I'd like you to think about the very first value you can remember having—and how old you were.

- "Would some of you like to share?" (Write down their responses.)

Reflect on some of their responses as they fall into different categories, e.g.– "So some of you learned to appreciate that value when . . ."

Trainer's Note: While most of the people will probably mention positive experiences, some may mention negative experiences that showed them why a value was important—for example, when someone lied about them, they learned the importance of honesty. Note their experience in a few words on the flipchart. You may want to question further to find out if, at the time of the experience, another person took the time to discuss honesty with them, or listened to them, etc. Ask:

- "As children, what would you like to tell the adults of the world? What would you like them to do; how would you like them to treat you?"

Record their responses on the flipchart as you repeat or paraphrase what they say.

Say, "I think you have just described a values-based atmosphere."

Facilitator's Note: Say the above sentence if they have just done that. Based on previous training, the participants usually say such things as "listen to me; love me; respect me; let me play; give me limits," etc. If they have not described a values-based atmosphere, simply summarize what they have said.

Say, "As educators, we know that children readily learn. The Latin word for educate means to educe: to bring out, to develop the potential which already exists. Educating about values is rewarding for children and teachers, and it gives us the opportunity to help create that better world."

Optional Activity:

Give the participants paper and crayons. Say, "Please express a feeling about something you have just experienced. You may wish to draw, write a poem, put down one word or make a splash of color—whatever you wish that expresses a feeling about a value."

Session Two: Exploring Our Values as Teachers

Trainer's Note: Different facilitators have different styles, and participants have different needs. Two options are given below for a second Values Awareness Session. Select one of the following two options, or create your own values activity.

Option A, Mind Mapping

Ask the participants to select a value that is important to her or him and find other participants who feel that value is also important. Ask them to form small groups and Mind Map that value. Demonstrate on a flipchart how to Mind Map if they are not familiar with that technique. You can find instructions in the Appendix of *Living Values Activities for Children Ages 8–14* or *Living Values Activities for Young Adults*. Or, if many participants choose the same value, ask some of them to create Mind Maps of the value, and some to create Mind Maps of the lack of that value, or anti-value.

Option B, Processing Values

Prior to this session, place a list of the twelve values featured in LVEP on a flipchart or use Overhead 1 from the History and Overview set.

Begin the session with the activity "Past, Present and Future Values." Please refer to Introductory Activities in the prior section.

After the introductory activity, say, "Living Values: An Educational Program focuses on twelve universal values. I would like you to pick two values as a group, and then tell me what those values mean to you and how they have affected your life."

- Ask the group to select two values. (This activity can be done with the entire group. However, if there is a large group, it may be better to break into small discussion groups.) Write the values on the flipchart at the top of the page (in two columns) and then ask for each value:
- "What is _____? What does _____ mean?"
- "Remember a time in your life when you experienced this. Would anyone like to share his or her experience?"

Facilitator's Note: Be aware of the pace. Give sufficient time for them to respond to each question, waiting until at least three respond.

Say, "It is interesting that we share similar values. In the classroom, teachers automatically transmit their values to the students simply by their behavior. A teacher can model acceptance and patience, or impatience. A teacher can demonstrate enthusiasm for learning and regard for each student. A teacher models, with or without the intention, a way of being.

"Teachers influence what students care about and develop passion for. Teachers transmit their love of caring for the environment, their belief in peace; some transmit their enthusiasm about the written word or scientific inquiry.

"As human beings we all teach what we have learned as people, simply through our attitudes, words and behavior. Hence, it is important to know what we are conveying. This is part of what creates the atmosphere in the classroom.

"I'd like you to reflect on several questions." (Play some music.) "Please write down your answers."

- What values do you transmit to your students through your words?
- What values do you transmit to your students through your actions?
- What values do you have that you would like to model more than you are doing now?

Ask if anyone would like to share, and note the responses on the flipchart. The trainer can then make a reflection about the process: "In a group atmosphere of acceptance—of trust, caring and respect—we can express ourselves and see the self reflected in a way that we are not able to see individually. In an atmosphere of acceptance, each person is freer to learn and be creative."

3. CREATE A VALUES-BASED ATMOSPHERE

Session One: Rekindling the Dream

Introductory Remark

"I think most of us have a dream of how we want our school and classroom to be. That dream is part of the reason we choose to work with children. For a few moments, let's rekindle that dream and see what we come up with.

"Many of you have probably done visualizations before. If you have not, I want to say that visualizations have 'different languages.' Some people create pictures in their mind, others experience feelings and others use words. Simply relax, yet focus on my words." (Play some relaxing music softly.)

School Visualization

"Let your body relax and be comfortable in the chair where you are sitting. If you like, close your eyes (pause). As you relax, imagine a beautiful large bubble softly floating down next to you (pause). This beautiful iridescent bubble has a door, and a little sign that says, 'Step inside, and the bubble will float you to a better world—to the school of your dreams.' So, you step inside the bubble and the bubble begins to float (pause). It floats above this building and begins to travel (pause). You enjoy the scenery below you (pause). Gradually the balloon reaches the school of your dreams . . . and starts to descend (pause). As the bubble gently lands on the ground, you see a school nearby. You notice the building and the vegetation (pause). It is early in the morning, and a few students are starting to arrive (pause). You notice their expressions as they walk along the pathway and chat with their friends (pause). You slowly walk up the path, noticing how you feel (pause). A colleague greets you warmly as you enter, and you talk for a few moments (pause). What does he or she say? (pause). You walk down the path, noticing the environment (pause). As you approach your classroom, students walk up and say ___ (pause). You enter your classroom, looking around at the colors and the physical setting (pause). As the bell rings the students enter. You notice their expressions as they say good morning (pause). You start the morning, noting their attitude toward the lessons, and yourself as you teach throughout the day (pause). Perhaps there is a special activity you do, or something the students plan together (pause). You watch them work together . . . and with you during the day (pause). At break time, you walk out to the school grounds and see the interaction (pause). Picture the rest of the day in your mind (pause). And when you are ready, you wave good-bye and step into the bubble that is waiting for you (pause). The bubble floats up above the school . . . and begins to bring you back here . . . as you sit in your seat, the bubble disappears . . . and you bring your attention back to this room."

"Please share what you pictured." Write down their responses on a flipchart, noting their responses in separate columns for the environment, teachers and students. If you like, ask the following questions:

- What was the environment like?
- What did you feel like?
- What were the other teachers like?

Training Components

- How did the students behave?
- What were their attitudes?
- What did you enjoy about the students?

"Thank you. Now I'd like you to take a few minutes and pretend that you are a child in the school of your dreams." (Play some relaxing music softly.)

Imagine Being a Child in the School of Your Dreams

"Think about the atmosphere in the school of your dreams . . . the things you get to do in the morning and during free time (Pause for two minutes.) What is your teacher like? (pause). What does the teacher like to do? (pause). How does the teacher look at you? (pause). What is her or his tone of voice? (pause). What does she or he say to you? (pause). What kind of atmosphere is there in this school of your dreams? (pause). How do you feel as a young student? (pause). As an older student? (Pause for a full minute.) See yourself interacting with the other students (pause). What kind of projects do you get to work on? (pause). How do you feel in that classroom? (pause). In the school of your dreams, tell the children or your friends anything you want to tell them . . . and then slowly imagine yourself back in this room." (Allow thirty seconds of silence.)

"Please share what you experienced." Draw out how they felt as children in that school of their dreams and write down their responses on a flipchart.

If a participant states that they felt loved in that classroom, or safe (or other positive emotions), ask:

- What helped you feel that way?
- What did the teacher do that helped you feel that way?

Accept all answers and note them down on the flipchart. They may be one-word responses, such as: listened. You may wish to note all the feelings in one column, and the words, tones and actions that helped to create that feeling alongside it in the next column.

"Thank you." If you wish, comment: "We seldom put ourselves in the place of a child. When we do, we have a lot of wisdom to share."

Best Teaching Practices—Small Group Discussion

Ask participants to form small groups to discuss "best" or "optimal" teaching practices to create a values-based atmosphere. Depending on the composition, you may want to ask them to group themselves according to grade levels. Allow them at least fifteen minutes. Ask participants to provide feedback to the larger group. Thank them for sharing. Ask:

- In the optimal school environment you imagined as a child, and as an older student, did you feel—or believe it would be beneficial to feel—understood?" (Accept nods of head as an answer, and quickly state the next emotions.)
- Loved?
- Respected?
- Valued?
- Safe?

Content

There are nine overheads in chapter III which accompany this section. Put up the first overhead.

"Children are naturally curious, eager to learn, and have many beautiful qualities. They are creative, caring and can think for themselves. In a values-based atmosphere they bloom and thrive."

Put up the second overhead.

Say, "One of the premises of the LVEP Theoretical Model is that:

"Children do best in a learning atmosphere in which they feel loved, understood, respected, valued and safe.

"Several of the original educators involved in Living Values: An Educational Program took a look at values-based teacher attitudes and actions in relation to these emotions. The following overheads review some of their experiences over the years. It's an interesting way to 'frame' (to view from a different perspective) the best teaching practices."

Put up the third overhead. Say:

- Here in the middle, (pointing) is an emotion students experience in an optimal values-based environment.
- Here are examples of values-based teacher attitudes and actions that help create and support those emotions.
- On the right are values that help teachers sustain those actions—and model those values.

"Educators experiencing the emotions of their personal values seems to help educators deal with a common factor globally—stress."

Note some of the current stressors of the educators in the room: perhaps pressure regarding test scores from the administration, too many after-school meetings, etc.

"We cannot control many of the stressors outside of the classroom, but we can control the environment in the classroom. As educators, very often there is so much stress, we forget to 'be.' We become 'doings' instead of 'beings.' In that process, we lose most of what we enjoy about being in the classroom. When an educator focuses on staying in the experience of a value, much of the stress falls away. When people are in tune with their values, stress dramatically diminishes."

Show the overheads of the information below, briefly highlighting some of the information, and being open to questions, comments and discussion. Ask:

- "From your discussion on best teaching practices, is there anything you would like to add to enhance the likelihood of a child experiencing the emotions of being loved, understood, valued, respected or safe?"

Emotion: Feeling Loved

Values-Based Teacher Attitudes and Actions	Value
Attitude:	Love

In our classrooms, we can create an environment where
children, young people and adults can express themselves
and feel loved because of who they are—not only because
of what they say, have or do.

When I enjoy children and observe the process, I can stay
happy within.

Enjoying and believing in students allows them to accept
and believe in themselves.

Behaviors:
- Showing warmth, caring and kindness.
- Affirming the positive qualities in each child.
- Creating a healthy environment where children can grow
  and develop holistically, without favoring some students
  over others.

Emotion: Feeling Understood

Values-Based Teacher Attitudes and Actions	Value
Attitude:	Love

Each child is an individual with her or his own emotions
and process.

Each student can learn best when her or his emotions and
level of readiness are accepted and respected.

Behaviors:

- Listening.
- Giving students the space to express their feelings and ideas.
- Giving students the space to accept, and process with clarity,
  the answers to their needs and to situations.
- Listening openly, without expecting certain answers.
- Listening without expectations.
- Being open and flexible to students' ideas.

When not listened to, people often feel disrespected or insignificant.

Emotion: Feeling Respected

Values-Based Teacher Attitudes and Actions	Value
Attitude:	Respect

In the classroom, I can establish a climate of mutual respect
and understanding.

Behaviors:

- Listening carefully and attentively.
- Listening to what the student is really saying.
- Taking the time to recognize the emotions behind the words.
- Establishing classroom norms with the students.
- Setting limits and being clear when students are outside the norms.
- The educator's tone of voice in the classroom is consistent with creating a values-based atmosphere. According to the situation, sometimes the tone of voice may be caring, enthusiastic or encouraging; at other times it may be clear, firm or serious.

Emotion: Feeling Valued

Values-Based Teacher Attitudes and Actions	Value
Attitude:	Respect
I believe each student can learn and progress at many different levels.	Tolerance
I value each student and believe in her or his ability to understand and learn to be peaceful and happy.	
I am a facilitator of change. I have a clear vision of the task.	

Behaviors:

- Showing enthusiasm for the student and the task.
- Communicating high expectations through the belief in each student's ability to learn.

- Creating positive learning situations to help students understand and learn, accepting where they are.
- Present challenges and aims within their reach. Success increases their interest and boosts their confidence.
- Affirm positive change and actions, highlighting students' progress.
- Using nonverbal cues—a positive attitude, facial expressions and eye contact—which value each person, thereby generating enthusiasm and happiness in the student.
- Showing the ability to stay content and enjoy the process of students creating.
- Showing the ability to enjoy the student and stay calm inside even when the student is not "producing" as he or she "should."

Emotion: Feeling Safe

Values-Based Teacher Attitudes and Actions	Value
Attitude:	Peace
The classroom is a place where each one of us can experience dignity and being safe.	Respect

Behaviors:

- Treating mistakes as a source of information and a starting point for new learning.
- Asserting that no one is allowed to harm others, and no one will be harmed.

- Giving guidance in ways of being, how to behave, and what to do and not do.
- Generating understanding during discussions to help students make better decisions.
- Being consistent and clear about norms of behavior, and carrying through fair consequences for misbehavior in a matter-of-fact manner.

Answer any questions the participants may have.

The last overhead for this session contains the following:

Values are the brushstrokes that give meaning to our lives. They color human reality with new ways of understanding, creating in us the passion to carry out our plans. In our quest for excellence, we overlook the easy path, the one we all know inherently. Running through our learning process is the invisible path of feelings and characteristics. To lead students to travel this path, it is necessary to provide activities that introduce quality change not only in what students "learn" but also in what they "become."

—*Living Values Educators' Kit*

Session Two: A Tool Kit

Trainer's Note: "Spirituality" is a popular word in some cultures and countries, and is used frequently in school settings in those countries. In other countries, this word is unpopular within the school context, and looked upon with fear and suspicion.

While some countries include moral education as a daily part of the school curriculum, others strictly separate "church" and state, hence even the word "spirituality" is not used openly. Yet, we are all spiritual beings; it is the spiritual that unites us as a global family—it is what joins us behind the veils of religious differences—what will allow us to recapture our understanding of the value of each person, each culture and each religion.

This session on spiritual attitudes was created by people of different religious backgrounds in the United Kingdom. Only the trainer and the educational institute will be able to decide if it is appropriate for their setting, in their particular culture/government. In some countries it might be met with extreme resistance, in others it will be like a breath of fresh air. Should you wish to use it as a workshop, allow one and a half hours. The questions could be posed to participants, and they could discuss them in small groups.

A Tool Kit for Teaching Spirituality

How do you teach spiritual aspects of the curriculum? What do you do to ensure that you are addressing the spiritual component of the Spiritual, Moral, Social and Cultural? Ofsted inspections report on these dimensions of the curriculum and many teachers are seeking advice on what they should be doing. You may wonder if it is an element of religious education! Do you have to be religious in order to teach the spiritual area? Do you have to be a spiritualist in order to teach spirituality? Such questions are not uncommon in many staff rooms, which is why the following tool kit has been developed.

The tool kit was written following a series of meetings between three teachers and a sculptress: Linda and John Heppenstall, myself (Neil Hawkes) and Wendy Marshall. We explored the notion of spirituality in the context of West Kidlington Primary School's values education policy. The tool kit is designed to help teachers' spirituality—and explore how to develop it both in themselves and in pupils. I do hope that you will find our ideas for the tool kit helpful and, like us, see spirituality as central to your work.

Values Education

At West Kidlington we use the term "values education." This is a general umbrella term for a range of educational elements which is the foundation of our school. These include the following: values; behavior; personal, social and health; worship and spiritual; arts; and the statement on the principles of our values work. This is in response to the many requests for further information, particularly in the area of spiritual development.

Spirituality

The tool kit is a series of steps which enable teachers to develop knowledge, skills and understanding about spiritually. Before you start on these steps you need to be clear about what spirituality is and what it is not!

I find one of the easiest ways to understand spirituality is to think of it as your personal inner world of thoughts and feelings. A world that is real in the sense that it is your consciousness but cannot be seen. Only the results of your thoughts and feelings can be seen, in the form of actions which create the material world of objects, such as cars, clothes, entertainment and so on.

The purpose of teaching spirituality is to help pupils to be aware of their spiritual nature: their innate natural qualities through which they can lead more fulfilled and happy lives. This area of the curriculum is holistic in the sense that it deals with the whole person helping pupils to become more responsible for their thoughts and actions. The benefits for the pupil, school and community are significant and have, I believe, the potential to change our society for the better!

Suggested Spiritual Tool Kit

1. A clear understanding of what spirituality means

Begin to develop an understanding of your inner world of thoughts, feelings and emotions. This is your spiritual world. A clear understanding of your own spirit will enable you to develop an understanding of the concept of spirituality, which is at the heart of values education.

What Is Spirituality?

We are beings made up of body and spirit. We are aware of our bodies and a moment's thought will make us similarly aware that we are conscious beings, with ideas, feelings and powerful emotions. They are the essence of our spiritual world. We can think of ways to develop the physical body or the intellectual mind, but what about the spirit? If the spirit is not developed, we grow into incomplete adults in just the same way as if the body and mind are not developed; thus we will not be able to lead full and contented lives.

How can we begin to understand what our spirit is? Imagine a delicious chocolate with an almond center. The wrapping is like the body, attractive and eye-catching. The chocolate represents the conscious mind, and at the center, the nut, or nugget, is the same for everyone. It is the source of qualities and virtues such as love, trust, truth and peace: it is the higher self. It needs to be nurtured to affect the quality of our own and other people's lives.

We can appreciate that each of us has a spirit. It is possible to say, "I don't know your name, but I recognize who you are" as an acknowledgment of something we share, the higher self, the spirit. It is within each of us, and it shows that we are more than the everyday roles we play such as husband, wife or teacher.

2. Get to know your spiritual self

Quiet reflection is the route to this destination. Give yourself time to be with yourself, and begin to explore your spiritual self by sitting quietly in a positive way, focusing on aspects of yourself that create good feelings. Make sure to create thoughts and images which do not lead to a critical frame of mind. If negative thoughts occur to you, acknowledge them and ask them to move on so you can concentrate on positive ones.

Meetings with Yourself

Giving yourself regular, quiet, reflective times puts you in touch with your spiritual self, creates well-being and helps you to be in control of your life. During reflection, consider qualities such as humility, respect, responsibility, love. What do they mean? Are you aware of them within yourself? They are present but may be hidden. Over time you will reach your higher self, and know and appreciate your spiritual identity. The method is simple and only needs a commitment to put aside a regular time for practice.

3. Have a desire to grow spiritually

Getting to know yourself is hard work, a lifetime's journey. Be on that journey. The rewards are enormous as you become more objectively self-aware and self-confident. Your teaching will improve and be less stressful as you concentrate on the positive, rather than beating yourself up for perceived failures. Learn to praise yourself!

When you are on this journey, you consciously and unconsciously begin to show your inner self, your best self, to your pupils. You become a model for them, an example, and children recognize and respond to it. For instance, as you develop the quality of respect within yourself you may see your children differently, as equal beings sharing a learning experience with you. They will notice and respond with respect.

The more you heighten your inner, spiritual qualities, the more you will raise the self-respect and self-esteem of your pupils. This follows when you appreciate your pupils, you are honest with them and you trust them.

Without self-esteem there is no learning progress!

4. Communicate with others on a spiritual level

As you become more aware of your spiritual self, you will find you are more likely to communicate with others spiritually. You begin to see people at a level not dominated by appearance. You are less likely to think of people from the viewpoint of your own selfish ego.

How do we communicate with people? Usually at three points:

- appearance
- personality (emotion)
- spiritual

Communication via appearance is nice, but transient.

Communication via personality and emotion can be very nice, but can also be painful.

Communication via spirituality is what we all really want: a deeper, spiritual connection, unconditional love, acceptance. When you communicate with people at this level it will be evident in everything you do and say; it will manifest in your interactions and your relationships.

Communicating with Pupils Spiritually

When you communicate like this you will find that children respond appropriately without realizing why. They will have respect for you, they will consider you to be a good teacher, and you will find the job of teaching becomes easier and more fulfilling.

5. Actively teach others

Plan to develop the pupils' ability to work on all the steps given up to now. At West Kidlington School we do this through the process described in our Values Policy which describes how we raise academic and social standards by giving emphasis to:

- stillness—calm—reflection
- monthly values—well-planned assemblies—class reflection
- class lessons—stories that penetrate deep layers of human experience
- circle time—discussion of values—spiritual core

Conclusion

Developing the spiritual climate of the school, and hence values education, requires the commitment of the head teacher and all the staff. It follows that the head teacher must model values education for the staff, and indeed that the school as a whole must "walk its talk," as pupils are quick to spot inconsistencies! As a teacher, don't expect behavior from a child that you are not prepared to model yourself.

Benefits

The benefits are many, and include improved interpersonal and intrapersonal relationships; the latter being about the relationship we have with ourselves. Also, the quality of work is improved as a result of reflection and self-discipline. Pupils remain on task during lessons because of the conducive work-related atmosphere that is created; pupils are relaxed but alert and focused on their work. Listening skills improve, as do presentation skills.

Staff report impressive benefits to them as people, as they are less stressed and able to focus on good teaching. I hope that you will enjoy exploring the ideas contained in the "tool kit" and that the process will help you to develop a clearer understanding of spirituality. Good luck!

—Contributed by Neil Hawkes, Headteacher

Oxford, England

4. LVEP COMPONENTS

Session One: LVEP Theoretical Model, Materials, and the Variety of Values Activities

LVEP Theoretical Model

Opening Interaction

"We've been exploring values and discussing optimal school environments."

Draw plus signs in the shape of a large semicircle in the upper half of a large sheet of paper, or on the board, on which the following is already drawn.

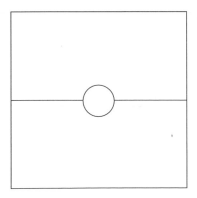

Say, "We've been defining some clear components of a values-based atmosphere. You mentioned . . ." Name some of the elements they contributed in the last couple of sessions and write them above the pluses. Such as:

- listening
- accepting environment
- encouragement
- clear limits and rules
- adults who model values
- mistakes seen as opportunities to learn
- an interactive learning process
- respectful relationships

Ask: "What else? What else contributes to a values-based atmosphere?" They might reply:

- conflict resolution
- peer mediation
- counseling
- building trust

Continue to add plus signs and the skills they name.

Say, "Student behavior can be positive or negative." Make a "B" with a plus and minus sign in the small middle circle.

"In this model, there is a commitment to dealing with all behaviors in a way that empowers students toward positive choices."

Content

Display the first LVEP Theoretical Model overhead.

Theoretical Model

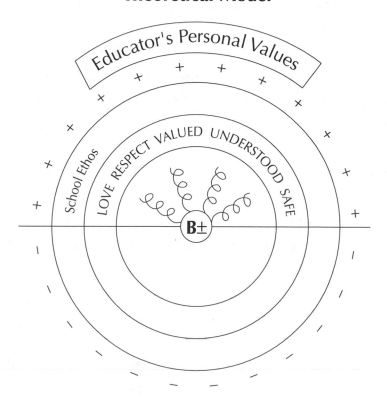

Say, "The LVEP Theoretical Model promotes the creation of a values-based atmosphere in order to improve the quality of education for the whole person. A values-based atmosphere can be defined as a caring, respectful, positive, safe space for a person to develop and learn. Such a learning atmosphere is encouraging, challenging, open, flexible and creative. A values-based approach is about creating activities that assist children in being at their best."

"The LVEP Theoretical Model promotes the creation of cycles of empowerment and excellence, through a values-based atmosphere. This model provides a means for examining cycles of inadequacy, hurt, fear, resistance, blame and anger in order to eliminate them. The intent is to positively improve the quality of education, and enhance student development of positive emotional and social skills through learning about universal values.

"In the last session one of the constructs of this model was mentioned: That children need to be loved, respected, understood, valued and safe; and that in such an atmosphere they are able to develop not only the intellectual dimension, but the affective dimension.

"Both creating and maintaining a values-based atmosphere can be challenging. It's easy with children who are secure and confident, who already have good social skills, and who enjoy school. One of the original motivations for doing this project was to reach not just the motivated students, but the 'unmotivated' students. Let's explore the cycles of empowerment or blame.

"What does everyone want? A basic human need is to be loved. If we cannot get love, then we want to at least be acknowledged or recognized. We all love to be appreciated for who we are."

Begin to make curved lines upwards, emanating from the small circle with the "B" as you mention each positive student behavior. Say, "When students are young, most are eager for the attention, love and praise of their teachers. We've all seen students who make effort and are polite. They naturally seem to receive more smiles and positive attention from everyone around them— and their good grades and continued adult and peer recognition reward their efforts. Their confidence builds in a good teaching environment as they are challenged and succeed. Others with good social skills usually continue to try for smiles and acknowledgment.

Training Components

"It's easy to respond positively and constructively when people are positive with us—and even easier when we feel appreciated and loved. It's easy to live those values.

"Most teachers can easily spot a child in trouble—readily identifying them even at very young ages—angry, depressed, already discouraged, feeling inadequate. Some children are already so discouraged entering school that they fear to try."

Negative Spirals:

Show the overhead of the LVEP Theoretical Model with examples.

Say, "When behaviors that interfere with the learning environment are dealt with in ways that increase the feelings of inadequacy, hurt, fear, shame and being unsafe, students do not thrive.

"Students come to the classroom in all states, some woefully unprepared, be it in terms of their language development, emotional readiness or behavior."

Make a downward curve emanating from the little circle in the center, or point to the same place in the overhead of the LVEP Theoretical Model with examples.

"If a student feels inadequate (trace along a downward curve), and meets further failure (touch the juncture in the curve), he or she is likely to feel more inadequate (continue tracing along the downward curve). When that student is given disapproval or rejected by a peer (touch the next juncture) he or she is likely to feel worse. Motivation decreases and less effort brings more failure.

"Some students become resistant to learning, and feelings of inadequacy and hurt cycle into depression. Others cycle into hurt, fear, resentment, blame, resistance, anger and sometimes violence." Ask:

- "What are factors that keep a negative spiral going downward"?

Make minus signs in a semicircle on the lower part of the flipchart as the teachers supply answers, such as:

- negative home environment
- shaming, blaming
- belittling, sarcasm
- low entry level of language skills
- little individual or small group help when needed
- yelling, shouting
- negative peer remarks
- scapegoating, ostracism by peers
- inadequate nutrition

Ask: "And how do we feel as educators when students are disruptive?" Perhaps the trainer can share a personal story here of an experience as a new teacher that he or she now finds humorous.

The teacher participants may share some of their feelings. If they do not, comment: "Sometimes, some educators feel anxious or inadequate when students in the class are disruptive. Blame, resentment and anger can follow. An interplay of these emotions between student and teacher can increase a downward spiral. Angry voices and punitive measures affect everyone in the classroom. The students who are acting negative act worse. Controlling through fear or anger isn't what educators want to do. It not only ruins our experience, it increases anxiety, and learning and personal growth are inhibited. Anxiety interferes with students processing information and learning. This ensures less success.

"In the following skill sessions we'll look at keys to avoid creating the emotions that fuel the negative spiral. It is as though negative emotions such as inadequacy or resentment collect other negative emotions. The emotions of being valued, loved, and respected seem to collect other positive emotions within the self."

Show the overhead of the LVEP Theoretical Model. Point to the upper inner larger circle with the words: LOVE, RESPECT, VALUED, UNDERSTOOD, SAFE. Say:

"These are the emotions viewed as the needs of children in this model; keeping these emotions in mind helps us evaluate the methods being implemented within the educational setting."

• Point to the middle larger circle with the words: School Ethos. Say:

"Educators at each site are encouraged to think about the school ethos they want. What are three to five values or qualities that are most important to you for your school/site?"

• Point to the top arch with the words: Educator's Personal Values. Say:

"Each educator can reflect on the core values that are most important to her or him in the educational setting. Selecting three values to experience during the day is a tool to decrease stress, and naturally model values."

• Point to the lower inner larger circle. Say:

"This space is for emotions that distance children from their potential and continue a negative cycle or spiral. Negative factors in the environment tend to produce the emotions of INADEQUACY, HURT, FEAR, SHAME and INSECURITY."

• Point to the middle larger circle. Say:

"What is the School Ethos is this case? It could be 'Motivation through fear.' Or 'Control through punishment.'" (Pause for any responses.)

Training Components

This model provides a framework for schools, educational settings and individual educators, to examine the positive and negative factors within their setting in order to increase the positive cycles and decrease the negative spirals. Entire schools can assess and look at their setting, educators can assess the classroom environment or school guidance teams can use this model to help them explore what factors are affecting a particular student. They can discuss:

- What are the positive factors that exist within the setting?
- Do we want to strengthen or increase those?
- What are the negative factors?
- How can we decrease their impact? Through training? Through positives that will transform the negatives?
- Are there positive factors within the community that could help us?
- What adjustment of existing methods and resources would make this more effective?

To deal with negatives, for example, older students who are misusing their positions of control over younger students could be trained to use positive methods instead of those that generate shame and fear.

If negative home environments are a factor, it might be constructive to involve parents in parenting classes.

If inadequate nutrition is a problem, the community might be involved for a short- and long-term solution.

In the sessions that follow, we will be exploring skills to create a values-based atmosphere. The methods of discipline, for example, are designed to avoid perpetuating the negative cycle while moving the student toward consideration of positive choices and skills.

Educators have created many positives—sports programs, homework clubs and mentoring programs are a few. We have not talked about the variety of values activities. These are also "pluses"—assets in helping students develop personal social and emotional skills for life.

Materials

Trainer's Note: Information on the 1997 and more recent edition of Living Values Educational materials are found below. Review only the edition the participants will be using. Appropriate overheads can be found in the History and Overview set (Training Component 1). You may want to discuss in detail only the books the participants will be using.

1997 Edition
Living Values Educators' Kit

Section One: Setting the Context—Offers an introduction to and history of the Living Values: An Educational Initiative. An abstract of the kit components is in this first section.

Section Two: Commitment to Values-Based Education—Delineates the commitment to values-based education by the various partners and consultants involved in Living Values: An Educational Initiative. There are messages from UNICEF representatives, information on the consultants, and the names and addresses of the initial educators involved.

Section Three: Educators' Manual—An English translation of a ninety-one-page Spanish publication entitled *Valores Para Vivir, Manual para Educadores*. The Educators' Manual provides ideas, proposals and experiences to promote working with values within the educational community. Guidelines for activities in the classroom and the need for creating enabling environments to share and experience values are explored. Teachers from different continents have shared their experiences experimenting with values-based education in both formal

Training Components

and informal learning settings. Evaluation is presented as the art of knowing, understanding, learning and creating. It explores the challenge of ideological change both within the educational system as well as with educators—a necessity for comprehensive and global values-based education.

Section Four: Blueprint for Values-Based Curriculum—In this section, suggestions are given on how to approach values-based education in schools: factors to consider, and what and how to evaluate.

Sections Five, Six and Seven: Values Activities for Children and Young Adults—The next three sections contain a variety of values activities for children at different age levels. They are grouped in modules for children, ages two to seven, eight to fourteen and fifteen to eighteen.

Section Eight: Parents/Caregivers Module—These facilitated sessions are designed for parents and caregivers to further understanding and skills important in encouraging and positively developing values in children. Please see the *Living Values Parent Groups: A Facilitator Guide.*

Section Nine: Appendix—This section contains stories and a conflict resolution sheet for use with the Living Values Activities for Children and Young Adults.

Section Ten: Evaluations—Two forms are included for completion by the educator and the older participants.

Section Eleven: Train-the-Trainer—Information was given about the initial Train-the-Trainer programs.

Section Twelve: Children-at-Risk and Refugees Module—This section for children-affected-by-war is a unique series of activities that give children an opportunity to begin the healing process while learning about peace. Please see *Living Values Activities for Refugees and Children-Affected-by-War.*

Living Values Card Pack—Inspired by *Living Values: A Guidebook,* these forty-eight cards are designed as a tool for teachers and students to explore inner values. Each of the twelve values has four cards, one with point for reflection, a second with a suggestion for a discussion, a third with a suggested activity and the fourth with a method to practice.

Living Values Poster—This 8½-by-33-inch poster can be used as a header for bulletin boards, decoration at a values fair or simply to designate a space for values. The twelve values in LVEP are written in blue on white glossy paper.

Current Six Books

The content of the original *Living Values Educators' Kit* was expanded and separated into six books in 1999 and the early part of 2000.

LVEP Educator Training Guide

This book combines information from the *Living Values Educators' Kit* with the experience of educators who conducted Living Values Educational Training Seminars in twenty-one countries during the first phase of the program. It offers potential LVEP trainers information about LVEP; sessions designed for educators to explore values awareness; creating a values-based atmosphere and skills for creating such an atmosphere; and materials. Sample training agendas are offered for one-, two- and three-day educator trainings and a five-day train-the-trainer session.

Living Values Parent Groups: A Facilitator Guide

This book offers both process and content for facilitators interested in conducting Living Values Parent Groups with parents and caregivers to further understanding and skills important in encouraging and positively developing values in children. There are three sections. The first section describes content and activities for an introductory session and a six-step process for the exploration of each value. In this process, parents and caregivers reflect on their own values and how they "live" and teach those values. The second section offers suggestions regarding values activities the parents can play in the group, and ideas for parents to explore at home. In the group sessions, parents play the games their children will play and learn additional methods to foster value-related social and emotional skills at home. In the third section, common parenting concerns are addressed, as are particular skills to deal with those concerns.

Living Values Activities for Refugees and Children-Affected-by-War

This program for children-affected-by-war is a unique series of activities that give children an opportunity to begin the healing process while learning about peace. Daily lessons provide tools to release and deal with grief while developing positive adaptive social and emotional skills. The separate series of activities for ages three to seven and eight to fourteen contain many of the lessons included in the Peace, Respect and Love units of the Living Values Activities for Children section. There is also a section on Camp-Wide Strategies, offering suggestions that could be implemented in refugee camps. This includes strategies to create a culture of peace, values education groups for parents/caregivers, cooperative games and supporting conflict resolution monitors.

Living Values Activities for Children Ages 3–7

Children at this age level naturally develop values-based behaviors in a values-based atmosphere. The activities include circle groups with discussion and reflection on values, but primarily offer the opportunity to enjoy and explore the values through *Quietly Being* exercises, stories, songs, games, movement and other values activities. Activities for interpersonal social skills development, including conflict resolution, are included. Educators can send for cassettes of songs to accompany the book. Some activities are appropriate for children two years of age.

Living Values Activities for Children Ages 8–14

A "teacher friendly" book, Living Values Activities for Children Ages 8-14, contains goals and objectives, scripted daily values lessons, stories, games and ideas for a Values Fair. A variety of activities are used to involve students in exploring and developing values at an intra- and interpersonal level.

Living Values Activities for Young Adults

A wide range of issues and personal and emotional skills are broached in this program in order to involve students fifteen years and older in an enjoyable but serious exploration of values in relation to the self, others, their society and the world. Please see the Goals section of Living Values Activities for Young Adults for a complete list of goals and steps toward achieving those.

The Variety of Values Activities

Trainer's Note: If the participants are educators of just one age group, refer to the introductory section of the Living Values Activities book they are using for a description of the variety of values activities. An overhead master is available.

Content

It is not enough for children to simply hear about values. To really learn, they must experience them at many different levels, making them their own. It is not enough to feel, experience and think about the values; social skills are needed to apply values in interactions throughout the day. The students of today increasingly need to see the effects of their behavior and choices, and develop decision-making skills that take into consideration the needs, rights and viewpoint of those around them. If the youth of today are going to carry these values into their personal lives as adults and into society, then it is also important to have them explore issues of social justice, and have adult role models who exemplify those values.

The variety of values activities with the LVEP materials have been classified as follows:

Reflection Points

Reflection Points are at the beginning of every value unit and are incorporated in the lessons. They define values in simple ways for younger children, and offer more abstract concepts to older students. In addition to defining values, the reflection points offer a universal values perspective, that is, of valuing the dignity and worth of each human being and valuing the environment. For example, points in the Respect unit for ages three to seven are: Respect is knowing I am unique and valuable and Respect is knowing others are valuable, too. A Tolerance Reflection Point is: Tolerance is being open and receptive to the beauty of differences. Many of the points are taken from *Living Values: A Guidebook.*

Educators are encouraged to add Reflection Points from the wisdom of the culture(s) of the community, and historical figures. Students can make up their own reflection points or research favorite sayings from their culture or history.

Imagining

A few values units contain Imagining exercises. For example, students at all ages are asked to imagine a peaceful world and share their experiences.

Creative visualizations not only elicit the creativity of "good students," but have been found to interest those students often considered resistant or "unmotivated." Visualizing values in action make them more relevant to students, as they find a place from within where they experience that quality and create ideas that they know are their own.

Relaxation/Focusing Exercises

Very often students do not like "having to be quiet" in school. They may experience it as curtailing their fun and repressing their energy and enjoyment, something necessary to do in order to comply with adult requests. The Peace and Respect units introduce Quietly Being exercises to children three- to seven-years-old, and Relaxation/Focusing exercises to older students. These are designed to help the students enjoy "feeling" the value, and to teach a method of nurturing the self. Teachers have found that doing these exercises helps students quiet down, de-stress, and concentrate more successfully on their studies. After several values units, students are asked to create their own Relaxation/Focusing exercises.

Artistic Expression

Children are encouraged to reflect about values, and make them more of their own by experiencing and expressing them artistically and creatively. They make slogans about peace and put them up on walls, for example, and sculpt freedom, draw simplicity, and dance cooperation. Little children make wings representing humility and self-respect, then sing a related song as they do a circle dance. During the value of simplicity, students are asked to take short walks in nature, write a poem to a tree and have the tree write one to them. While some songs are within the material, educators are asked to bring in traditional songs of their culture, or the cultures present in the area, and sing those with the children. Older students create poems and songs about values, and bring in their favorites.

Self-Development Activities

In these activities, students explore the value in relation to the self, developing personal emotional and social skills. For example, small children use puppets to express words and behaviors that would be in a peaceful world. Students of all ages explore their qualities during the Respect unit, and their feelings about honesty and dishonesty. There are activities to increase self-respect, the belief that "I make a difference," to discern the difference between dignity and bragging, to learn encouraging self-talk and increase responsibility. Please see the goals for more information on the numerous self-development activities.

Social Skills

These are activities where students explore values in relation to others, developing interpersonal communication skills. Some of the activities include learning conflict resolution skills, exploring how to apply peace, respect and love to beginning conflicts and situations that the students are concerned about, discerning subtle and not-so-subtle ways respect and disrespect are given and developing communication guidelines after playing cooperation games. Please see the goals in each *Living Values Activities* book for more information on the numerous activities for developing social skills.

Cognitive Awareness of Social Justice

There are activities for preteens and young adults to explore values in relation to the society and the world, with the aim of developing awareness about and commitment to values in order to contribute to the larger society with respect, confidence and purpose. They mind-map respect and honesty, and discuss science and its purpose. Some of the activities for young adults include exploring the effects of greed and corruption: examining the consequences through skits in relation to the history or social studies curriculum; researching the relationship between corruption and the denial of human rights; and applying values in discussions about business, economics and government. Please see the goals for more information.

Developing Skills for Social Cohesion

The units on respect, love, happiness, cooperation, tolerance, simplicity and unity contain activities to explore and develop values in relation to the society and the world. Children make "happy boxes" to practice different virtues throughout the day at school, while young adults are asked to set up an experiment to create an "Accepting Environment" at school. Activities for older children and young adults include those that aim to increase understanding of the importance of values; awareness and skills for tolerance and social responsibility; communication skills to build the feeling of unity; and environmental awareness and responsibility. Please see the goals for more information on the numerous social cohesion activities.

Incorporating Values into the Existing Curriculum

History, social studies and literature lend themselves easily to an exploration of values, as do the arts. Teams of teachers can brainstorm values applications at their particular site, or in their subject area.

These Values Activities Are Only a Beginning— Incorporate the Values of Your Culture

It is our hope that these activities will elicit ideas from teachers and parents as they explore with children the variety of ways to experience and explore values. This material is intended to be a stimulus. Use your own resources and creativity. Bring in stories, songs and games from your culture, and the cultures within and around your country, to illustrate values. Have the students create their own plays, songs and assemblies. Perhaps older adults can tell traditional tales and teach ancient forms of music.

5. VALUES ACTIVITIES WITH EDUCATORS

Session One: One or More Sessions

Values Activities in Teams

In this part of the training, educators are divided into teams to experience some of the Living Values activities. In most trainings, coaches act as teachers with the teams. Recommended team size is from ten to fifteen participants. However, twenty-five participants in one team have been very successful.

The trainer will note in the Sample Training Agendas that the shorter trainings have less time for the educators to experience the values activities. Hence, some have just one short session, while others have three sessions. TTTs can be designed with four values activities sessions.

Factors to Consider

Age Groups

The trainer will need to know in advance the ages of the students with whom the participants are working. Sometimes educator trainings will be for one age group. Often, however, there is a need to do more than one age level. In a primary school training, for example, coaches will be leading activities from *Living Values Activities for Children Ages 3–7* and *Ages 8–14.* There are three age levels for the purposes of the training, correlated to the age ranges of the *Living Values Activities* books.

- Children, Ages 3–7
- Children, Ages 8–14
- Young Adults

Divide the participants into age groups of their students and arrange at least one coach for each age group.

An Experiential Approach

There are different ways of approaching educators when introducing Living values activities. The approach taken in this manual is experiential. Coaches actually do the values activities with the participants; the coach assumes the role of teacher and the participants are asked to simply enjoy the activities, allowing themselves to be in a childlike state of mind.

Values Activities Teams and TTTs

During TTTs, the trainers and coaches have another option to consider: Will the participants be training educators at all different age levels? If this is the case, divide the participants into teams, and give each team the opportunity to do values activities at each of the three age levels.

In a recent training, for example, there were six teams and six coaches. The coaches taught activities at the same age level for three sessions while the teams rotated. Then a fourth session was held in which team members experimented with teaching the values activities. In the fourth session, allow each team to split in half so that more participants can have the opportunity to teach an activity.

Training Components

Coaches

Ideally, coaches will be educators who have taught the values activities, are very personable and are able to model the creation of a values-based atmosphere. The facilitator/trainer of the entire training should meet with the coaches to go over the training and describe the process.

Ask the coaches to select the activities they wish to do in advance of meeting with their team. Suggest that they include a variety of living values activities, that is, a reflection point, an imagining exercise, a Quietly Being exercise or Relaxation/Focusing exercise, songs or a dance, an activity that requires team interaction or social skills, and artistic expression. Ask coaches for young adults to take part in an activity that involves a social justice issue.

Ask the coaches to select activities from two values units.

In a One-Day Training, Do Values Activities on Peace and Respect

If the training is to be for one day, begin with the values activities units on peace and respect.

During Values Activities Time, Do LVEP Activities

Using Living Values activities helps participants become more familiar with the contents of the program. Participants should have a copy of the *Living Values Activities* book at the beginning of the session. Coaches are advised to review a few points from the book with the team prior to leading the activities.

Next Sessions: Processing the Experience, Sharing Ideas for Assemblies

Processing the Experience

After doing the values activities, each team remains together and does the "Next Session." The coach is to ask participants to share their experiences. Encourage them to process any of their questions or concerns. Then generate a discussion on ways to make teaching values practical in their particular settings. Other topics may include time slots in which to teach values, strategies and ideas for assemblies and integrating cultural activities. Schools with daily values lessons usually do one value a month, beginning with an assembly. Schools doing less frequent values lessons may need two or three months on a value as the lessons should be done in order.

Sharing Their Experiences: An Exposition

After teams of educators have done the values activities sessions, they can share with each other by having an "Exposition." Each team can set up the paintings, crowns, puppets, slogans, alternative tolerance words, mind maps, etc., that they have created during values activity time in a designated area.

Of course, if it is a small training with only one team of teachers, there is no need for an "Exposition." However, if there are multiple teams focusing on one age group, or teams rotating to all three different age groups, the trainer is advised to allow a space in which they can share their creations.

If the training has offered all three age levels, and participants have only been able to experience one age level, you may wish to allow some "Exposition Time" as well as space. The teams may wish to have one-third of its members rotate to be with the exposition, and others seeing the other teams' materials. The members who stay with the exposition may share thoughts and feelings about the activities, recite a poem or demonstrate an activity. At the end of the time, a couple of teams may want to invite everyone to join in a couple of songs or a dance.

Alternately, it is fun to arrange a "cultural show" where each team can present an item or two that they did while in their age group.

6. SKILLS TO CREATE A VALUES-BASED ATMOSPHERE

Session One: Acknowledgement, Encouragement and Building Positive Behaviors

Content

Say, "For a few moments, I want you to think back to your childhood, and remember:

- the ways you were acknowledged or encouraged; (Pause for a few moments.)
- the positive things people said to you or about you. (Pause for five seconds.)

"We remember the positive things our parents told us, and the negative. When we are children, we tend to repeat in our head the things that are said about us. We believe them. We know we have the good qualities they said we had, and that we are good at the things they said we were good at—and we have to work hard as young adults (or even mature adults) not to believe the things they said that we were bad at!

"Humans affect each other in every interaction. What are effective ways to encourage and build positive behaviors?"

Building Positive Behaviors

Trainer's Note: It is useful to illustrate the points below by drawing ascending steps on a flipchart like the diagram below.

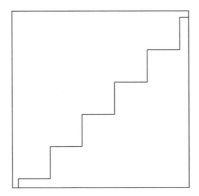

Positive Reinforcement Increases Behavior

Contingency Management teaches that positive reinforcers increase behavior. When a person experiences something positive for a particular behavior, that behavior increases. You may have a high goal for a student—mark a "Goal B+" (Positive Behavior) at the top of the stairs—but if you want her to achieve that goal, start with the current behavior. (Mark a "B+" on a middle step.)

It is important to find an appropriate (positive) behavior to reinforce. For example, if a young student has poor handwriting, try to find something on his paper to reinforce. Notice that in an approving way. For example, say in an interested and pleasant manner, "These letters are touching the line," or "You're putting the sentences together very well." This is especially important for students who have had little success in the classroom. Those who are achieving and doing well socially are already receiving many positive reinforcers in terms of good grades, teacher and parent approval and positive experiences with peers.

Create an opportunity to "catch them" doing something well. For example, ask the student to do one part of a task after you know they understand it. Or, ask a student to help you with a task or do something for someone else. Then, thank them or note positively what they have done.

Praise is usually a positive reinforcer. You can tell if your praise or affirmation is a positive reinforcer for a student by watching to see if the behavior improves in the direction of the goal.

So Why Doesn't Praise Always Work?

Some students don't seem to like praise and look sour when they get it. Their behavior certainly doesn't improve. Perhaps they found the praise embarrassing. Sometimes students don't accept praise. They simply do not believe you—perhaps you said it was "great" and they do not think so.

A few children occasionally get worse immediately after excessive praise, as they are so accustomed to getting negative feedback that the positive feedback is anxiety-provoking. The child may try to stop the anxiety as soon as possible by doing something negative. (Make an arrow going down the steps on the flipchart drawing.)

If you give praise, and the behavior gets worse, you know it is not acting as a positive reinforcer for that child.

A Few Simple Rules for Building Positive Behaviors

Trainer's Note: You may wish to note the five points below on a flipchart in advance.

1. Give Believable Praise, Make It Specific.

While a child with a good self-concept who is accustomed to praise will react pleasantly to a glowing comment, students less accustomed to praise will often reject positive general comments as unbelievable. If your praise is specific, they can verify that it is true. For example, a five-year-old will be pleased and believe your saying, "You made the back of that 'D' straight and just the right size." He can observe the "D." He may not believe your saying, "You have the best printing in the world." Or, you may want to recognize a student's effort with a classmate: "You listened to Guillermo when he really needed you to listen. That was being a friend." Or, "Wow, this group knows how to cooperate."

"Specific praise" is not necessarily praise—the positive may be conveyed only in the adult's attitude and voice tone. The words can be descriptive.

Specific praise is an excellent instructional tool in that it can point out key variables important for the successful completion of a task. For example, "You remembered a topic sentence at the beginning of that paragraph," or "I like the way the darker colors flow from one side of the painting to the other."

Specific praise can be used as a step in helping students develop intrinsic motivation. When a student asks you if something is good, and you know they have been receiving specific praise—so they know some key variables important to the task—give her or him a smiling look, indicating that it is good and say, "You tell me what's good about it."

2. Give Specific Praise, and Name the Quality.

Examples of this are: "I liked the way you just helped Nannette. You were giving happiness." "You didn't hit him when he called you a name. You stayed in your self-respect and power. Good for you!" Or, "I appreciate you volunteering to help with that. You are so cooperative." Or, to a young child, "I like the way you thought about it and were able to stop and say 'arms are for hugging, not for shoving.' That was choosing peace."

Students remember what qualities you say they have. Your recognition of their qualities can be very important. It can begin a change for those who feel inadequate—altering their self-perception from negative to positive. Knowing one's own qualities is an important foundation for self-respect and self-esteem.

3. Be Genuine.

As human beings, we instantly perceive feelings. The words can be classified as those that give acknowledgement, encouragement or praise—but to have a positive effect they must be genuine.

- How do you feel when someone gives you praise and you think they don't mean it?

It is your affection and love that are important to a person—those feelings give students the experience of being valued, and permission to appreciate their own work and efforts. We are all human beings. Love, recognition and being valued are what people want. Taking delight in a person, appreciative eye contact, and respect are invaluable indicators of sincerity, easily perceived by two-year-olds, eighteen-year-olds or forty-eight-year-olds. A simple appreciative glance or a "thumbs up" signal may be the best affirmation for some students.

A three-year-old girl with a just-finished painting is quite happy with a description accompanied with smiles and loving eye contact: "Wow, look at all the colors you used—red and blue and purple! And there are all sorts of circles and lines!" That specific description actually has no "praise" in it at all, but acts as a positive reinforcer as the child feels valued with the affection received.

Occasionally, there are teachers who are frustrated with classroom behaviors who believe they are giving praise when they angrily say, "I like the way this side of the room is quiet." Human emotions are the most important part of the equation. Anger invites resentment and retaliation. How do we function in an atmosphere of anxiety, control by fear and resentment? . . . We survive, but do we bloom? There's no substitute for real appreciation and love.

4. Praise and Encouragement Always Leave a Positive Feeling Within the Receiving Person.

Sometimes people really try to praise or encourage, but end their comment with a "spoiler." For example, how does the husband feel when the wife says, "Honey, you did a great job cleaning the garage. It looks so organized. I don't know why you don't keep it like that all the time. It's always such a mess! . . . " That was a spoiler! Or when the husband says to the wife, "What a delicious dessert that was! Why can't you make something like that more often?" Or when the teacher says to the child, "You concentrated and finished your work quickly. Good job. If you'd only do that all the time, it wouldn't be such a hassle every day." The comment started out well, but when the comments turn to nagging or reminding others of past negative behaviors, the positive feelings usually diminish quickly.

Effective and true acknowledgment, encouragement, recognition and praise leave a pleasant feeling in the mind. We need to communicate with students—what is the effect of each of our remarks? Even clear rules, high expectations and limits can leave a feeling of hope in the mind.

The delivery of your positive affirmation must adapt to the receiver!

We speak differently to people of different ages. With students as well, it is important to vary the tone of voice and manner of delivery according to the age and personality of the student, and your relationship. Cooing is great for babies, gushing for most two- to four-year-old girls. Some young children prefer a few quiet words or a happy glance. Boys tend to prefer praise delivered in a matter-of-fact way, especially after age nine. Watch their reaction to find if they are accepting of specific praise, but shy away from flowery words.

Many teenagers are like soft-boiled eggs: hard on the outside, soft on the inside. They may not seem to notice your praise—may shrug it off the hard exterior—but you know it has been effective when that behavior increases, when they want to spend more time near you and when the hard facade on their face fades. Initially give the "hard" students dry, matter-of-fact praise ("Not bad!") or a little note. You can gradually increase the open positivity of the praise as they soften. Watch for a change in their behavior—if they are approaching you more and the behavior is growing in the direction of the praise, it is being received as a positive.

5. When a New Behavior Is First Beginning, Praise It Immediately.

It is appropriate to provide immediate feedback for a new positive behavior. A few students will not work unless there is someone at their side. Consequently, they usually get very little done. Provide them with a new behavior by doing the first problem with them, then saying, "You know how to do that. Great! When you have done these three, hold up your hand." Make a mark at the end of the third problem. When you go over to reinforce him, increase the amount of problems he is to do before you come over again. Within a short time, the student will be working much more independently and getting much more done.

While frequent praise is often needed in establishing a new behavior, as the behavior becomes a habit, gradually reduce the praise. Occasionally you might praise the continuing effort. For example, say with a smile, "You've been remembering that homework every day."

Session Two: Open-Ended Questions and Active Listening

Open-Ended Questions, Acceptance and Acknowledgement

Content

In Living Values Activities for Children and Young Adults you will find open-ended questions during or after many of the values activities. The open-ended questions encourage students to think about a concept or process and then express their thoughts and feelings. If students are to really develop values, they need to explore their emotions during different activities and connect with them. In an active discussion they are free to explore different alternatives, and discuss concerns that are real to them. They can apply presented skills and concepts, debate them and learn from each other in the process.

It is essential for teachers to be able to use open-ended questions as an effective tool during the Living Values activity classes. That requires the educator to not just ask the questions, but to accept and acknowledge students' answers, and at times generate other questions. The most critical skill, however, is nonjudgmental acceptance.

Acceptance and acknowledgement of students' responses is an essential component of many discussions that take place as part of the values activities. This may pose a challenge to teachers who are accustomed to having only "right" or "wrong" answers in the classroom. While there are "right" and "wrong" answers in math and science, a student's emotional feeling about a concept is his or her own. People feel how they feel.

While sometimes we may wish that children (and certain adults) did not feel a certain way, not to accept their emotional response is to invalidate them—to act as though they do not have a right to their emotions. To reject a person's feelings is to push him or her in that direction; acting to increase attachment to his or her attitude. To accept another person's emotions does not mean that we agree that he or she "should" feel that way, it simply means that we understand the feelings and accept that that is how the person feels.

When the listener accepts the person and the feelings, an opening is created to explore, and for the student to move toward more positive, and healthier, perceptions, emotions and behavior. Instead of feeling invalidated, being understood and valued allows the person to accept his or her own self. Movement in a positive direction is then possible rather than defending his or her own feelings in what feels like defense of the self.

It is wonderful to watch children who are unaccustomed to acceptance of their creative thoughts and feelings. In one pilot of LVEP, the teachers noticed that the students noticeably grew in self-confidence and motivation. They observed that the students were delighted at being able to create, and their answers being accepted and genuinely acknowledged.

Dealing with Resistant Nonstandard Responses

Resistant students may initially test the acceptance of their answers by giving nonstandard responses. For example, when asked about a peaceful world, a student might say, "War has to be part of a peaceful world." Or, in response to a question in the Happiness unit about what he or she likes to hear, a student might respond, "I like to hear that I am horrible." Simply consider these responses as reflections of the student's unhappiness. Nod with respect, just as you did to the other students.

It is sufficient to nod, but a verbal response, acknowledging their answer and restating the content of his or her message, is a more effective method of giving respect. Consistently receiving respect from an adult in this way frees the student from the trap of blaming the adult for not understanding. Actively listening to such responses allows the student to accept her or his emotions, and begin to process them. For example, if the student draws guns in her picture of a peaceful world, the teacher might say in an accepting, genuine and serious manner, if the student's face seems tense, "It must be scary if there are guns even in a peaceful world."

You may wish to add your own positive answer or state why you feel a certain way at some point in the lesson. Students are generally curious about teachers and are often interested in a teacher's passion for something noble/good/true. When this is done, resistance usually fades, and the student's natural qualities begin to emerge.

When Students Insist They Are "Bad"

Sometimes students may insist that they like something or someone that harms—for example, they may choose to admire a negative figure. If this has come up during a discussion (it might be better to do one-to-one if the students like to make a show for his or her peers) ask, "Why do you admire that person?" "What do you think that person would like to see happen?" "Why?" "What is the value under that?" Continue to query, focusing closer and closer to the original intention.

There is always a positive value or quality under the original intention. When this is done, the teacher can affirm, "So, you admire _____ _____", making note of the positive value. This is said with the understanding that people do wrong things, but somewhere there is a good motive. It may not be well thought out, it may have disastrous consequences for other people, but somewhere there was a good intention. The purpose of taking this approach with a student is to align him or her with a positive value or positive purpose. They can change their own view of self as "bad" if there is acceptance of a positive value or caring about something. Nurture that kernel in positive ways, and the student can begin to view him or herself differently.

Students are encouraged to think, look at consequences, and develop emotional awareness and problem-solving skills in this program. Allow them space to explore and make their own decisions. Then they will make wiser decisions—and not only when adults are watching!

Time for Reflection

Open-ended questions are also used to explore what students think after they are given a couple of minutes to reflect on a Reflection Point. The use of some silence, or quiet thinking time while some soft music is playing, is an enriching experience for many students. Giving them a little space to explore their own thoughts, after having given them something positive to think about, allows them to get in touch with their own positive thoughts and feelings, and is often a springboard for creativity.

Active Listening

Content

"Often teachers and other adults who deal directly with students feel frustrated or helpless when young people feel badly about peer problems, or when they are upset with their friends, family, coaches or teachers. Many educators are skilled listeners and make time to discuss alternatives with students. Most teachers have little time to listen; when they do, many give direct advice. Others may sympathize or admonish.

"Think about when you are really upset with someone, perhaps you are crying, and another person jumps in, immediately telling you what to do. How do you feel? (Pause for their response.)

"Or, they tell you how silly you are being. *'You shouldn't feel that way. Don't be silly. Now, what you should do is . . .'* How do you feel, better? (pause).

"Picture that same scene over, but this time the other person says, *'You really are upset right now.'* And sits down to chat with you and listen. How do you feel? (pause).

"What do most people do instead of listening?" You've listed some of them: giving solutions, diminishing. What else? (pause)."All of these things block the communication."

List the following on the board or use the overhead. Discuss.

Blockers and Stoppers

1. Accusing
2. Admonishing
3. Blaming
4. Diminishing
5. Distracting
6. Giving Solutions
7. Judging
8. Moralizing
9. Sympathizing

"Patient listening on the part of a caring person is an invaluable gift. Reflecting feelings allows others to accept and 'own' their emotions."

"Anger is a secondary or tertiary emotion. Hurt and fear are the primary emotions underneath. At times shame or concern about safety can also be underneath. Anger is never a primary emotion."

ANGER

hurt, fear, shame, unsafe

+ +

+ + + +

+ +

Facilitator's Note: Draw the above diagram. The drawing above the word "ANGER" represents flames. The +'s are each person's positive core values and qualities.

You may wish to refer to the Three Core Assumptions overhead, pointing to the middle one. Say:

"Each student cares about values and has the capacity to positively create and learn when provided with opportunities. One of the assumptions of the program is that underneath all the other behaviors and emotions, each student has positive core qualities and values."

Give a couple of examples of the primary feelings of hurt, fear, shame, or feeling unsafe, moving toward anger, for example, when a loved one is several hours late, or you are called a name.

Training Components

Give an example of anger being a tertiary emotion. For example, a parent becomes angry because he or she is embarrassed by his or her daughter's behavior. The secondary emotion is embarrassment. The primary emotion underneath the embarrassment could be fear for the daughter's future, shame that the daughter would behave in such a way in front of someone else, or fear that he or she is not a good parent.

Then say, "As emotions are accepted, they gradually reduce in intensity." For example, a child will frequently move from anger with an authority figure, to talking about how his or her feelings have been hurt, when someone actively listens.

The process of being listened to allows people to feel valued, to accept their own hurt and to look at the overall situation with more understanding. If there is a trusting relationship between the teacher and student, often one active listening sentence such as, "You seem really upset," is enough to move the student from anger to receptivity.

How to Actively Listen

Active listening is an effective tool. Active listening is:

- reflecting back some of the content;
- reflecting back some of the emotions that the other person is communicating—without sounding like a parrot;
- listening genuinely.

It requires taking some time, and having an accepting, caring attitude. If you listen with your heart, all the nonverbal cues will automatically be accepting.

Be careful about imposing your feelings and reactions about what they are saying. Instead, simply listen. Occasionally reflect back some of the emotion or content, at other times nod or acknowledge with a little sound. It does require practice to do this in a way that is genuine and natural.

Group Practice: Before you break the participants into groups, give a few examples of active listening. Then the trainer can give several sentences that the participants can "actively listen" to.

For example:

"My friend hits me hard sometimes." Possible active listening responses depending on the person's nonverbal cues:

"You don't like it when he hits you."
"You feel really sad when he hits you."
"You feel anger when he hits you."
"It sounds like your feelings get hurt as well as your arm."

Active Listening Activity: Ask participants to break into groups of three. In each group of three, have them count off one, two and three. For Round One: Person One will be the talker, Person Two the listener and Person Three the observer. See chart below for "round robin" assignments.

	Person 1	Person 2	Person 3
Round 1	Talker	Listener	Observer
Round 2	Observer	Talker	Listener
Round 3	Listener	Observer	Talker

- For Round one, two, and three, each "Talker" is to share something positive that happened to her/him.
- Do this again, this time asking each Talker to share something that is important to her or him or something that makes her or him feel peaceful.

- Do the three rounds again, if there is time, this time asking each Talker to share something that he or she feels angry or sad about.

During each round, the listener should be encouraged to use active listening skills, occasionally reflecting the feelings or emotions of the talker, restating the content of the message. The key to active listening is really listening to what the other is saying and not projecting one's own thoughts and feelings into the message. The observer in each round is to provide feedback.

Open up the meeting for sharing of experiences and questions.

When to Problem Solve and Give Advice

"Sometimes the question arises, 'I want to give advice. When is the best time?' If someone is upset, listen first. After someone has been listened to, and feels valued or more in touch with their primary emotions (away from the anger, the secondary emotion), they are clearer and consequently more open. Then, a little advice may be accepted instead of rejected. Or, there is an opportunity to say, 'What other way could you have handled it?' As students are encouraged to think and generate alternatives, their understanding of the process and their ability to think on the spot will grow. The likelihood of acting in a more positive way increases."

When Can I Listen, and When Is it Best to Not Listen?

"Listen when you have time; not when you don't.

"Listen when you can listen with love. If you are out of emotional energy, tell them you would like to talk with them later.

"Know your limits; if you can listen with patience for only five minutes, let the person know you only have five minutes."

Training Components

Close the session: You may wish to ask the group to share the values that emerged during the active listening experience if there is time.

Session Three: Transitioning to Values-Based Discipline

Opening Remarks

"In every country around the world, teachers are concerned about increasing levels of student disrespect, misbehavior and violence. Some teachers say that students do not listen to them, others that students continually talk. Others talk about student aggression. In some schools, students and teachers are not safe; they are hurt. The changes in student behavior mirror changes in society.

"In this session, we will explore some useful methods that contribute to and maintain discipline, and how to use those methods as part of creating a values-based learning environment. There needs to be balance. If there is no order, it is not possible to have a values-based atmosphere. Values-based approaches can be used to create order and harmony."

Content

"In societies around the world a percentage of youth are on the fringe. Why do kids move to become part of a gang or part of a group with a culture of violence? They are looking for a 'family,' a place where they can be accepted, protected and can achieve. Often, their home environments are less than nurturing, and they are less successful than others in getting positives from school—because their achievement is poor and their behavior inappropriate. With affection and approval from adults so rare, many find negative behavior the surest means of getting some attention.

"When negative behaviors are frequent, they are a signal of a child's need to connect and be recognized as real. However, frequent angry behaviors also spring from the hurt of not receiving love, and hence are retaliation against adults. If a nurturing adult connection is not possible, such students still try to get that recognition, praise or acclaim—but it is usually from peers who are heading down the same path."

"One key is to generate cooperation through collaboration and ownership. Let's explore how behavior norms, that is, classroom rules, can be established in a collaborative way, and the importance of communicating high expectations to students. These work together hand-in-hand."

Rules and Expectations

Establishing Classroom Rules Collaboratively

It is essential to have classroom rules or norms of behavior. It is not essential to establish them collaboratively. However, the process of doing so can be great for both students and the teacher—building a cooperative relationship and increasing students' sense of ownership. It can be part of creating a values-based atmosphere. Additionally, this way students learn communication skills and skills for cognitively exploring why certain rules are important. During the first couple of weeks in class, the teacher may also want to include students in other decisions—such as how they would like the classroom to be organized and what they would like to do.

A collaborative method of establishing "Guidelines for Student Behaviors" or "Classroom Rules" is to lead students in a discussion about rules they would like in their classroom. Involve them in decisions about what the norms will be. For example, open a discussion with: "This is our classroom. I would like you to be part of establishing class rules. What do you think our rules should be?"

Training Components

If you are starting Living Values activities, do the first couple of lessons in the Peace unit. After the Imagining a Peaceful World exercise is done, lead the students in a visualization of a peaceful classroom another day. After they share their experiences, ask them what rules or norms they would like for their class.

Listen to what they say and help them put the rules in a positive form.

If a student offers, "No hitting," or "No name-calling," you might say, "Can you put that in a positive sentence, not using the word 'no'?" or "Give me a sentence that says what we want people to do." Give them examples as needed while acknowledging suggestions by repeating the essence of what has been said. For example, "So, you would like one rule to be 'Respectful behavior to others.'" Or, "You think everyone keeping their arms and legs to themselves is a good rule." And, "You think one rule could be 'Positive language to each other.'"

Ask the students to create three or four rules or norms, no more than five. The teacher may want to add one that is obviously missing. Share with the students why you would like to add that rule. Post them in the classroom. They could even be on separate posters made by students—one for speaking, one for listening, one for studying and one for action.

The teacher must be comfortable with all of the rules.

If the students are testing limits and suggesting rules that are not possible, be honest, letting them know that there are certain things that are not permitted. Be clear about the limits. Share your reason if you are comfortable doing so. For example, "I think respect for each other is one rule that is essential. It gives you the freedom to achieve and the safety of being able to try—and it gives me the freedom to enjoy you, and teaching! Respect for everyone is one rule that must exist in class. Harming others is not okay, and is not permitted."

Sample Rules or Norms Are:

- Respectful hands.
- Listen.
- Work quietly during quiet time.
- Give respect to others.
- Treat everyone like you want to be treated.
- Play in a friendly way.
- Respect yourself and others.

Review the class rules after a week to see how everyone thinks they are working. Adjust them as needed. Compliment the students on the ones they are doing well. You may wish to schedule an "Our Classroom" review every week. You can review the rules and involve students in generating others as they progress—now that the initial norms they adopted are part of their classroom behavior.

Problem Solving

If new negative behaviors evolve, ask the class to create a new norm to resolve the issue. Sometimes the teacher may wish to have the students problem solve at the time when a behavior occurs. For example, if several people are talking at the same time during a class discussion, the teacher could say, "It is hard to hear everyone when there are several people talking at once. How can we talk and understand each other?" Ask the students to come up with a suggestion. If a student offers a method that the teacher knows will not work, acknowledge the suggestion (such as positively stating, "That's one idea") then query as to the consequences. ("What would happen if we did that?") Get the students to explore the ramifications of their ideas, both pro and con. The teacher can then ask, "Is this what we want?" "Is there another solution?" "What else would we like to see happen?" "This we cannot do. If you like we can try something else and return to this later."

Expectations

Teacher expectation messages are very important.

A belief that each child has positive potential and can learn and progress is essential for the well-being of the child. Expectations coming from this belief help students believe in themselves. Positive teacher expectations that communicate respect for students and belief in their ability to learn help students have more emotional energy. In turn, they focus more, are more motivated and are more open to learning. Ask:

- What expectations do you have for your students? (Write down their responses on a flipchart.)

Trainer's Note: Often you will hear two categories of responses; always mentioned are the behaviors students should have. Sometimes mentioned are teacher messages to the students, such as, "I want them to try their hardest." If you hear both types of responses, list them in two separate columns on the flipchart: Student Behaviors, Teacher Messages. Repeat their responses as you write them down.

Other positive teacher expectations are (mention those not stated already):

- I think you are capable.
- I know you can do a good job on this.
- I expect you to try your best.
- I expect you to work hard and do your best.
- I know you will be able to learn a lot this year, and do very well.
- I know you can respect yourself and others.

Think of messages you feel will motivate your students—positive messages about their ability to learn and do well, positive messages about their efforts and what they can achieve. Communicate these at the beginning of the school year or when you are changing to a values-based system—and then continue to communicate positive messages throughout the year. It is your caring behind these messages that makes them effective.

Acknowledge, praise or encourage their efforts: "You really put in a lot of effort—that's terrific." "I'm noticing how this team is planning so carefully—with such planning your project will be a success."

Of course, the teacher must create a positive academic learning environment to help students learn, and accept where they are. Present challenges and aims within their reach.

Presentation Style

The presentation style of the teacher will depend on the personality of the teacher, but also on the classroom behavior of the students. If the students in the class have a history of not listening and walking out when they wish, the teacher will need to have a much sterner, dry style than with students who are receptive. In such a class, it is still very important, perhaps even more important, to communicate high expectations. However, the teacher must connect with something that that group of students finds relevant.

Encourage

Recognize when they are having difficulty and encourage them to persevere in a positive way. "I know this assignment may seem a bit long. It is longer than the last one, but I think you are ready for it."

Stopping the Cycle of Negativity

Subtle Signals

Most teachers will try different subtle signals before implementing an action to stop a negative behavior. When a student is beginning a behavior of concern, teachers sometimes simply make eye contact, glance at the student so that he or she is aware that the teacher is observing, change the pacing, ask a question or move near the student physically. With a good relationship between the teacher and student, often a little smile and a glance is enough to have the student become aware again and control the behavior of concern.

A Peaceful Quiet Signal

Another way to cut short actions that the teacher would like to stop is to instruct the students to focus. A simple method is to develop an effective quiet signal, and then use the silence to have the students experience one of the values the class has worked on. For example, the teacher could say a few sentences about focusing in and filling the self up with peace or self-respect. This is easy to do if the class has been participating in the Quietly Being or Relaxation/Focusing exercise in the *Living Value Activities* books.

Teachers in some countries say that the students never listen to them, and are never quiet. A few guidelines for developing an effective quiet signal follow.

Find a symbol for peace and silence that the students like or have been having fun with. (This can be done during the first couple of lessons of the Peace Unit.) For example, with little children hold up the Peace Star. Ask the older students to come up with a peace sign they would like. You might want to play music for a minute, or simply wish to hold up that old-fashioned hand! If the class is noisy, it is more effective to verbally ask them to look at you, such as, "Everyone, look up here," or "Boys and girls, look up here, the Peace Star has come for a visit." With older students and adults, "Everyone, I'd like you to look up here. Let's focus." With older classes you may wish to drop the nonverbal signal after a while, simply saying, "Let's focus."

A major difference in a values-based approach is feeling full of peace when you give your signal, and continuing to stay in that state while you wait for everyone to be quiet.

If you speak or begin your activity before everyone is quiet, some are learning that they do not need to be silent when there is the signal. Wait for everyone, even if it takes a few minutes. Stay in a peaceful place yourself, and thank them. With little children, you may want to have the Peace Star add a comment about how he (or she) likes that. Comment positively when the time it takes to become silent becomes shorter.

Time-Out

Time-Out is a method used when students are disruptive. It is not considered a punishment according to the theories of contingency management; it is simply considered the withdrawal of positive reinforcement. The student is temporarily removed from the activity or classroom.

Time-Out works on the assumption that there is something positive available within the environment. The positive reinforcement may be the teacher's attention, or it might be attention from peers, enjoyment of activities or intrinsic motivation.

The principal reason for implementing an effective Time-Out system is that when it is working well, there is no need for punitive measures. This fits in well with a values-based approach, as the goal is to get out of the cycle of feelings of hurt, inadequacy, failure, blame, resentment and retaliation.

Training Components

Negative remarks can serve to increase negative behavior.

As people, most of us have been negative with others at some point in our life, yelling at someone or another for something. As educators, we are aware that people who use negative words and shouting as a constant method have real problems—with their own children and in the classroom.

An interesting study was done with parents some years ago. It was found that when parents gave more than twenty seconds of negative attention to a negative behavior, it acted to positively reinforce the negative behavior. That is, the negative behavior that they wanted to decrease, actually increased when the parent shouted at the child for more than twenty seconds.

In some countries, caning is still used. Yet studies have shown that the negative behavior diminishes only temporarily when a child is physically hit; within three days the negative behavior increases.

It is easy to understand this when we look at the affective dimension. As adults and children we can respond with hurt or anger when a lot of negativity is received. When there is physical or emotional punishment, resentment increases. When this occurs frequently, some people are not only angry with the punisher but become determined to retaliate. The retaliation may be overt, seen through a disrespectful, negative attitude, negative words or violence. Or the retaliation may be subtle, seen through diminished effort and deliberate failure.

When implementing Time-Out, it is important to use it as a values-based method. Too often Time-Out is used incorrectly; it has been used in a way that shames students. It then acts as a punisher that perpetuates rather than breaks the negative cycle.

Introducing Time-Out

Below is a suggestion for introducing a values-based Time-Out when there are still some discipline problems. A signal is suggested, as when students are being disruptive or disrespectful, the teacher wants a very quick way to stop the disruption—before it becomes contagious.

The teacher can introduce Time-Out by saying something similar to the following, modified, of course, to the age of the students. "In this classroom, I expect you to learn and do well. We've been talking about the kind of classroom we want to have, and class rules. If someone is not following those rules, I will give you this signal. (The teacher may want to touch her or his temple, tug his or her ear, make a snap sound with his or her fingers, or point to the Time-Out area.) That means that you are to sit over there (or stand outside, go to room #—choose a place that will work in your setting) for _____ minutes and think about what you could do or say that would help you and the class. If you are not following the rules, I know you are not feeling your best and need some time to think. We all have days when we don't feel so good."

A serious, firm and clear teacher attitude is best when introducing this to a class with a history of behavior problems. For an older student, start with five minutes.

Transitioning to a more values-based Time-Out—Thinking Time

Once the values activities are being done, and Time-Out is working easily, the teacher may wish to drop the signal, simply noticing when a student is having difficulty and approaching her or him individually to say, "You seem upset, would you like to take a few minutes?" Or perhaps, "I'd like you to take a few minutes in the Peace Tent."

You may want to talk to the students about naming a "Thinking Time" place. It could be the Thinking Time Place, Peace Corner or whatever sparks their imagination. They could decorate a place or make a tent.

Communicate About Behaviors of Concern Individually

Sometimes when working with students who have had chronic behavior problems, it is effective to dialogue with them and think together about ways to help them not get into the identified negative behavior. Begin the individual chat by telling the student what you like about him or her, what the behavior is that concerns you and why you think it would be of benefit to change the behavior. Sharing in this way, once there is a values-based atmosphere, is very effective.

Sometimes students benefit from the suggestion that they take a self-regulated Time-Out when they need it. Or, when you see that they are starting to go into their cycle of behavior, you can give them a preestablished signal to help them notice. They can then become more aware and decide if they want to change their behavior. They need to know that if it continues they will have the consequence, that is, be timed-out.

Time-Out with Younger Students

Time-Out is effective with children as young as eighteen months. The Time-Out period usually ranges from part of a minute up to fifteen minutes. Longer than fifteen minutes has been found to be ineffective. The cycle of resentment is activated.

For young children, you may want to establish Time-Out as a time to think about how to give happiness, and have a Peace Bear in the corner that will "help" the child think. For little children, start with one minute and gradually increase the time until the child sits for three to five minutes. For little children, a place nearby where they can see the teacher is often best, as it is less frightening.

Sometimes little children do not Time-Out easily. Make Time-Out less "scary" in their eyes. Explain to them that this is a time to think about giving happiness.

Practice doing a Time-Out when they are feeling good. Lead them gently by the hand. Practice filling the self with peace or a pink bubble of love.

When you do ask them to think for a moment, be calm rather than angry. Make the Time-Out place fairly close to you, make sure it is well lit and safe, and decrease the time to a few seconds of his or her being quiet. Gradually increase the time as they begin to Time-Out easily.

Help Them Create Alternative Behaviors

If the teacher can find time to chat with a student at the end of a Time-Out, one question could be, "Were you able to think of a way to do that differently?" Positively remark on the student's alternative. The insight and wonderful alternatives that children and young adults can produce are remarkable!

Stay Calm and Clear

In a values-based Time-Out, the teacher stays clear about the class rules and the importance of adhering to them, and tries to stay peaceful. **It is important to "Time-Out" students before you are annoyed or angry.** Anger fuels the negative spiral. When Time-Out is used without shaming or embarrassing, it becomes a time to think about how to be at their best. Time-Out students in a matter-of-fact manner. It should be based on their behavior, not on the teacher's mood. If you do it calmly, they will Time-Out easily.

If You Do Get Angry

If you do get angry with a student or the class, tell them about it. Share. For example, "I got really angry at you because I thought what you did was mean. Sarah's feelings were really hurt." If you acted in anger and have changed your mind, explain. For example, "I was so angry that I gave you a really big consequence. I think the consequence I gave you was too big. So, instead . . ." Being real with students, in a way that is appropriate for their age and maturity, is greatly appreciated by them.

This type of sharing, when the relationship is a safe and trusting one, builds even more trust. However, this is not the case for an adult who frequently vents anger at others and is angry most of the time. Usually the frequency of anger has created an anxious environment; trust has not been built into the adult-child relationship.

When Older Students Are Having Difficulty—
Consequences and Communication

Sometime there are students who will not initially Time-Out. During Time-Out, students are to remain quiet and not call out. If an older, regular student will not Time-Out, then consequences need to be added immediately in order to get her or his attention. For example, if a student is calling other's names in a loud voice in class and will not Time-Out quietly in the classroom, send her out of the classroom and then confer with the student later.

Use that time as an opportunity to learn about the student and hear her or his concerns. Does she or he need help with something? Does she need a tutor or a quiet environment in which to study? Listen to what the student has to say. Ask her about what she would like. Ask her to come up with alternatives that she might try. Allow her the privilege of giving you a signal when she knows she needs a Time-Out to think and quiet herself down. Encourage her best behavior.

If there is still difficulty timing out, confer again. Ask the student what consequences there could be if there is not compliance with Time-Out. Usually he or she will generate much harder consequences than the teacher would— hence, the student may see you in a new light when you tell them you think a lighter version of the consequence is sufficient. Ask the student about his or her goals. Together, generate a list of positive consequences for adhering to the class rules, and list the negative consequence that will happen if the behavior occurs again. Examples of negative consequences might be a conference with the principal, a conference with the parents, or losing a school privilege. Encourage his or her best behavior, and carry through with these consequences if the behavior occurs.

More serious consequences may be necessary for more serious behaviors. Create logical, fair consequences—and try your best to keep your own anger out of the equation. When the adult is not angry, and the consequences are logical and fair, students will begin to look at their own responsibility rather than blaming the adult. Let them know the door can be opened by appropriate behavior.

Students who have had a lot of rejection in their lives can really change with the above approach when the teacher continues to be firm, give regard and not respond to their anger. It may take time, but it does work. Creating a space of respect and caring allows people to change in a positive direction.

Session Four: Conflict Resolution

Facilitator's Note: A small percentage of schools use conflict resolution. It is a wonderful method to use with students and teach students to use with each other to resolve problems. If the school(s) you are conducting an LVEP training with already has a conflict resolution program, this session will not be necessary. However, if it does not, but you assume administrators naturally know conflict resolution, you may wish to do this session. While most people feel they can do conflict resolution, once asked to mediate a session, a high percentage have been observed to engage in guilt inducement, moralization, blaming and other behaviors that are counterproductive to students accepting responsibility.

Training Components

Session Material and Process

Present the information in the Peace unit of *Living Values Activities for Children (LVAC)* and *Living Values Activities for Young Adults (LVAYA)* during this session. There are Teacher Notes prior to the lessons on conflict resolution in at each level, as well as lessons.

LVAC Ages 3–7   Peace Lesson 12

LVAC Ages 8–14   Peace Lesson 15

LVAYA   Core Peace Lesson 8

Post the questions asked during the conflict resolution exercise on the board or flipchart. Mention that there are fewer questions for younger children in the conflict resolution process in *LVAC 3–7*. This is because little children do not usually insist on telling you what has happened. Indeed, often the problem is resolved as soon as they tell you how they feel! While a conflict resolution mediator would not normally suggest solutions, this is not strictly true when working with toddlers. They may need a little help with ideas of appropriate social skills.

Review the following rules for conflict resolution with the participants, and then model a couple of conflict resolutions. Then revisit the "Blockers and Stoppers" from the section on Active Listening, showing the difference.

Rules for Conflict Resolution for Mediators

1. Ask the questions in the conflict resolution process.
2. Listen carefully to each student.
3. Actively listen to students.
4. Direct students to listen to each other and not to interrupt.

5. Encourage students to listen.

6. Encourage students to repeat what the other student said.

7. Appreciatively note their ability to listen and communicate.

8. Avoid taking sides.

Blockers and Stoppers

1. Accusing

2. Admonishing

3. Blaming

4. Diminishing

5. Distracting

6. Giving Solutions

7. Judging

8. Moralizing

9. Sympathizing

Rules for Students Who Want Help with a Problem

1. Be willing to listen

2. Be willing to work on a solution

Practice

Ask participants to divide into groups of four, with two of the participants role-playing students with an unresolved problem. They may wish to take up a problem that occurs among their students. The third participant is to be the teacher who mediates the problem. The fourth participant is to observe and provide feedback, helping the mediator not to slip into the "Blockers and Stoppers." Continue to practice, allowing each participant to take a turn in each role.

Afterwards, ask them to share their experiences and invite any questions.

7. THE PROCESS OF EVALUATION

The Ongoing Process of Evaluation

Evaluation can be done in many ways, and it can take many forms. In this section, educator Pilar Quera Colomina shares her ideas about the ongoing process of evaluation in the classroom. As an educator, it is important to be aware of the interactions, making small adjustments to the flow—creating a meaningful way for the self and for each child.

You can't prepare your students
to build the world of their dreams tomorrow,
if you don't believe in your own dreams now;
you can't prepare them for life,
if you don't believe in it yourself;
you can't show the way
if you are stationary, tired and disheartened,
at a crossroads.

—Célestin Freinet
"Tutor of Adolescents"
J.J. Brunet and J.L. Negro Failde
Ediciones San Pio X, Madrid, 1982
Taken from Living Values Educators' Kit

Content

Whenever we question how we value what we learn, as educators we search for different strategies and practical resources that help students. In order to deepen the awareness and experience of one value, it is necessary to know the connection between what is happening in the present and what we want to learn. It is also important to understand the feelings and emotions that emerge.

The content of the event or knowledge has to have a personal meaning. Thus, in the evaluation, the observation cannot be focused only on actions and words expressed externally, but on the attitudes implied in the actions and words of others. This informal evaluation of an ongoing process is subjective in nature, and hence needs to include factoring in your own thoughts, emotions and feelings.

Values help children and adults alike. They make them peaceful, give them breathing space and provide them with all they need to improve: respect, self-esteem and recognition. They help them to understand themselves better—the difference between "being" and "doing." A way is thus facilitated to enjoy the newness of learning skills and knowledge, which was inaccessible or unattainable before.

In evaluating learning that takes place in a values-based atmosphere, it is necessary to relate the acquired achievements with the values that are being experienced; to see the values that emerge as well as the ones that are necessary; and to learn together to value, acknowledge and build the values at the core of the situation of each moment.

To have clarity in this understanding, the following three processes are helpful:

- Silence—the connection between us.
- Reflection and dialogue help us associate whatever has been learned with whatever we know and is meaningful.
- Visualization or imagining can help orient students and the teacher toward a goal.

Whatever is expressed externally germinates internally in the self. Silence facilitates an experience that leads us to reflect and to do the work of knowing ourselves from within.

The above three processes have been found to be beneficial in helping teachers and students:

- To live and experience the present moment
- To refresh the mind and experience serenity
- To be an observer; to increase our ability to listen to the self and others
- To increase the capacity of concentration
- To increase creative potential
- To restore the balance between what we think and do
- To increase the quality of whatever we do
- To rediscover our own values and qualities
- To express with confidence and security the values we have

Evaluation Is:

- the art of knowing, understanding, learning and creating.
- the process of communicating and helping students improve.
- a strategy that helps teachers plan and make practical adjustments in the classroom—for both students and teachers.
- the process of helping students emerge and develop within themselves constructive attitudes and values.

Training Components

It takes into account the learning process: Understanding the difficulties; the previous ideas; the attitudes; and personal factors.

Factors to Consider

- Positive, constructive attitudes
- High but realistic goals
- Self-confidence and trust in the self
- Enthusiastic attitudes
- Ability to be cooperative and caring
- Ability to communicate
- Ability to accept mistakes and continue forward

The above information can be found on overhead masters in chapter III.

More on the Process of Evaluation

An expansion of this information is available in the "Educators' Manual" (section 3) in the *Living Values Educators' Kit*.

In values-based education, evaluation is planned from a comprehensive perspective. Its aim is to improve the knowledge of reality and gauge the students' progress. But the reality in classrooms shows that evaluation is also used for other politics and ideals, such as hierarchical structures, control of behavior, selection processes, etc.

Any didactic process requires a revision of its results and effects, that is, an evaluation. Evaluation is useful for thinking and planning a didactic practice. Within a comprehensive values-based education, evaluation does not mean to measure, to quantify, as that makes it more complex. It answers questions such as how we can use the results from the evaluation or what is the aim of the conclusions. As José Gimeno Sacristán suggests: "Evaluating something or someone means estimating their nonmaterial value."[2]

Thus, evaluation is the result of constant observation, and it provides the information about the attitude we want to develop or about the value we want to know better, its degree of understanding and its application. This makes us think about the values underlying the choices we make and how to integrate, imbibe and develop them.

In values-based education, the evaluation should provide not only information, as stated above, but also a technique for the students to assess themselves.

We can target evaluation at different levels or groups.

First, there is self-evaluation of the teacher as an individual: the assessment of values transmitted while teaching, the process used, and the learning encountered and changes made.

Secondly, there is the evaluation of growth in a group of teachers and the application of values to the task of teaching at school. The evaluation of teachers is important because everything becomes possible and is made easier when members of the teaching staff in an educational institution work as a team, with a common vision and through research of the school's needs as a starting point.

It is also important to evaluate the students both individually and as a group.

Finally, we must evaluate the proposals submitted to see whether they facilitate the emergence of the values we are transmitting, to verify whether they are positive or they contribute to failure, and whether they lead to an environment of conflict or of collaboration.

So, how do we assess a process based on the development of values? We are referring to an evaluation process whose main objective is not to quantify

2. José Gimeno Sacristán and A. I. Pérez Gómez, *Comprender y transformas la enseñanza (Understanding and Changing Teaching)* (Madrid, Spain: Montana, 1992).

the results but to evaluate the quality of the process itself. We know from experience that the acquisition of values and attitudes is a slow and gradual process, especially if we want this process to involve qualitative changes or modifications. Therefore, a values-based evaluation requires the teachers to know they do not assess only results, but rather, they assess processes. Sometimes, in the short term, processes show no evidence of change.

We are proposing that evaluation be integrated into the mainstream of the learning practice, which starts from the beginning and continues throughout lifelong learning. This represents a new principle. This evaluation allows us in its initial phase to know the starting point of what both the student and the group think of the existing situations, as well as the ones which may arise in the future. This is essential information which enables us to make accurate decisions.

An ongoing evaluation as a feedback process provides data on what is being done and how it is being done, and gives an overview and analysis of the practice in order to review and improve it. It is also a strategy which leaves nothing to chance, and which helps us see the changes and adjustments which must be made during the process.

Once these questions have been identified in practice, we have to bear in mind that this ongoing evaluation will be formative. This is the most suitable method of intervention within the learning and understanding processes, both for the students and for the teachers. Instantly, we are able to observe and assess the situation, ourselves and the results obtained. We can see if the whole process is working as expected, if it interests the students, and if they understand the techniques and methods. In this way, we can approach the process again with this information: we can either put forward different pro-posals or continue working with the ones we had before. We must understand this implies a long process which will continue changing with time and practice. This kind of evaluation allows us to improve on our planning and interventions, since clear objectives are required to help understand the progress and the obstacles encountered by the students. Likewise, it allows us to put into practice situations, proposals and activities dealing with values that require cooperation between teachers and students. We can then define how they will be carried out through sharing and consensus, which implies the commitment of both teachers and students to the whole process. A commitment to play an active and responsible role in this process gives autonomy to everybody in such a way that tension is removed from situations because responsibility is shared. This helps us to observe if the class or group behaves with more respect in relationships and if everything takes place in a climate of harmony and happiness.

The process of ongoing evaluation only achieves pedagogic coherence if it is carried out by the teachers as part of their teaching work and includes monitoring the student's work in a climate of fluid and relaxed communication. The teacher should know the student's progress without having to set exams that have nothing to do with the student's daily work. In both values-based education and the comprehensive approaches to learning, it is not possible to separate teaching from evaluation. The evaluation is incorporated into the classroom process from the beginning, not just at the end.

When assessing values, we realize we are dealing in a complex yet enriching way with a process in which time is not a pressure, but rather a source of confidence in evolution and progress. However, in the short term we can see the results by observing the behavior of the students in the classroom; in the medium term, we can note the changes in the institution and the attitudes of the team; and, in the long term, the community can observe the behavior of the children and young adults in a wider context.

The students have to learn to assess themselves, to see the importance of values in their lives and in the formation of their personality. This self-evaluation allows them to see to what extent they have developed a personality based on values. To do so, first of all, the students have to define what their values are and decide which ones they would like to internalize and express as a person—in their relationships, when communicating with other people and in their lives in general.

Examples of Evaluation

There are different techniques for gathering data which can be developed, but one of the most practical resources is using the activity itself as a means of evaluation. In order not to limit ourselves to the field of intuition, we can use planning resources, control instruments or observations as well as the organization of information so we are able to verify it in practice. It is necessary to carry out an evaluation process that allows us to see the different ways of improving and reinforcing practices, the best strategies and the most effective activities, so that we become aware of our own progress. Also it is necessary to observe how the strategies work in different situations and the reactions of the students to change.

Developing teaching materials with the students and creating a simple and easy proposal make the students more aware of their own development. Simple tools can also be used, such as observation criteria, indicators of what to observe and control lists. All this can also be reflected in the students' work: in their textbooks, written essays, drawings, interviews, comments, surveys, sentence construction, reflections, expositions in the classroom, debates and personal journals.

Identify the Values

List of identified values	In which situations?	The most important ones. Why?

Ask students to exchange with one another their reflections about the values they have pointed out, to have a conversation about them. Then the entire class can agree on which ones they promise to practice. The agreed values can be recorded on a flipchart or board for the whole group to see them clearly.

These dynamics open up different options for evaluation in accordance with the desired objective. For example, if the objective is to gather data about the students' values, writing them down collectively on a flipchart or blackboard will enable teachers to see the aspects that are missing or can be complemented.

If the objective is to gather information about the integration or development of a value, an illustrative table designed for the individual can help the students put their reflections in writing and at the same time help to build a source of knowledge.

But, if the purpose is to gather data from the student's self-evaluation, then the following table is suggested:

The value I have discovered	Situations in which it is useful	When I recognize it: always, sometimes, never . . .

All these models can be completed and complemented with the different indicators to be observed and adapted to specific objectives.

A teacher can also suggest in the session a design for an evaluation model and then solicit the agreement of all; but such a process is not valid if all the participants do not agree to it. It is always more constructive to use interactive procedures such as interviews or reports which include the opinions of parents, students and the teacher.

Integrating values into the curriculum has a global effect. Values serve to develop specific attitudes within individuals in relation to teaching and learning techniques. As we have already seen, values can be identified in the behavior of the actual person and in relationships, as well as in more specific pedagogical activities. In the latter, we can recognize the influence of values in content matter, as they reinforce the work carried out in all areas of the curriculum. The development of values allows for greater adjustment and clearer understanding of these subjects. We can perceive this influence in the exercises which are proposed, as they enrich the basis of the knowledge that is applied in practical learning situations:

- The written essays improve because the values allow students to express their ideas more clearly as a result of concentration and attention.
- The enrichment of their oral expression is a result of sharing ideas and dialogues.
- The efficiency and accuracy of their work results from the tranquillity and concentration which they develop.
- The consistency and focused memory are necessary to acquire and retain concepts.
- The connection between concepts enhances understanding.
- There is a rising degree of attention, stability and independence.

All these factors are a result of more confidence, balance and inner stability, which are generated by instilling these values. These factors improve the quality of learning. We understand that values offer another educational perspective which allows for human improvement and cognitive enrichment.

At the beginning of the following school year, it is valuable for the teaching staff to decide which values have priority, taking into account their conclusions of the previous year.

A comprehensive procedure of global teaching and evaluation requires a change in ideology within the educational system as well as amongst members of the teaching staff. It also requires a more open and holistic mind-set when looking at educational priorities and developing the curriculum. This kind of teaching highlights new needs of the school organization in the approach to values-based education.

Training Components

Values content and academic content are not yet related in many countries. In the future, this concern should be emphasized and dealt with in a global context so as not to deprive individuals of true and complete development and lifelong training.

8. EVALUATION AND MONITORING FORMS

The following pages contain various Evaluation Forms for your use. Two of the forms are requested annually, in June.

Annual Reporting Forms

Reporting Form for Educators Using LVEP

This is an extremely important form. It allows *Living Values: An Educational Program* to receive input from educators about their experiences and the results of the program. We would appreciate educators filling this out every June.

Please send these to the LVEP coordinator for your country. They will send it to the International Coordinating Office.

Quantitative Report for LVEP Country Coordinators

Each LVEP Country Coordinator is requested to collect information annually.

Please send in this form to the International Coordinating Office in New York during June.

Optional Forms

Evaluation Form—Educator Training Workshops

This optional feedback form is for the use of LVEP trainers. It helps facilitators evaluate the strengths and weaknesses of the trainings they conduct.

Evaluation Form for Parents Participating in the Living Values Parent Groups

This feedback form is for the use of Living Values Parent Group Facilitators. Please send them in to your LVEP Country Coordinator who will then send them to the International Coordinating Office in New York.

Optional Student Evaluation Forms

Three optional feedback forms are for use by educators, to help them assess the benefits and needs of their students. Students can also give their feedback on the Living Values Web site.

Educator Reporting Form

Date: _____

Educator's Name: _____ Position: _____

Educator's School/Organization: _____

School Address: _____ City:_____

Country: _____ Phone/Fax/E-mail:_____

Month and Year You Started Using LVEP: _____

Please circle the edition you are using: Living Values Educators' Kit or *Living Values Activities* books

Who

What were the ages of the students you did LVEP activities with? _____

How many students participated? _____

How many educators were involved at your site? _____ Out of how many? _____

Did the entire school participate in a values program? Please circle: Yes or No

Values of Focus

Please circle the values you have focused on in the classroom/school.

Peace   Respect   Love   Cooperation   Freedom   Happiness

Honesty   Humility   Responsibility   Simplicity   Tolerance   Unity

Did you use SOME, MOST or ALL of the LVEP activities in the units you did? (Circle)

Did you incorporate values into the curriculum? _____

When

Values Activities, including incorporating values into the curriculum, were done:

Circle one: 5–20 min.   21–40 min.   41–60 min.   More than   Most of
                                                            1 hour   day

Circle one: Once a   Once a   Twice a   Three times   Daily
               month   week   week   a week

What percentage of the time do you feel there is a values-based atmosphere? _____%

Results

Please tell us about any changes you have observed in the students that might be attributed to their experiences in this program. Kindly approximate changes in the chart below, or describe changes. Please write in the percentage of students for which this is applicable.

90% of the students or ____% of the students	Good growth	A little better	The same	A little worse	Much worse
Self-confidence	5	4	3	2	1
Respect toward peers	5	4	3	2	1
Respect toward adults	5	4	3	2	1
Ability to resolve conflicts	5	4	3	2	1
Ability to cooperate	5	4	3	2	1
Responsibility	5	4	3	2	1
Honesty	5	4	3	2	1
Ability to focus/concentrate	5	4	3	2	1
Social skills	5	4	3	2	1
Interest in school/motivation	5	4	3	2	1
Overall school functioning	5	4	3	2	1

Please share any personal changes you experienced as a result of doing the program.

_____

_____

_____

_____

Is there anything else you would like us to know?

_____

_____

_____

_____

We would appreciate you sharing a "Success Story" below. Or, would you like to write one on the LVEP Web site? The address is *http://www.livingvalues.net*

_____

_____

_____

_____

Your students can put their pictures, poems, projects, etc. up on the Web site, too.

THANK YOU

Quantitative Report
for LVEP Country Coordinators

Date: _____

Name of Coordinator: _____ Country: _____

Coordinator's Address: _____

Coordinator's Phone/Fax/E-mail: _____

Dates of Pilot Started: _____ To: _____

Teacher Training

Please tell us about any LVEP Educator Trainings in your country. You may wish to include if it was a one-, two- or three-day training, and the number of teachers involved.

_____

_____

_____

_____

_____

What is the relationship with your country's Department or Ministry of Education, or other organizations?

_____

_____

_____

_____

_____

Schools

How many sites/schools were involved doing LVEP's Living Values Activities? Was the entire school involved at those sites, or one or two teachers? If you can, please indicate which cities or states the schools are in.

____ Day-Care Centers/Nursery Schools

____ Elementary Schools

____ Middle Schools

____ High Schools/Secondary Schools

____ Other organizations

Living Values Parent Groups

Please let us know if there have been or are Living Values Parent Groups, or if you are using the materials in other ways.

_____

_____

_____

_____

Any other thoughts? Anything else we should know? Did you use the Living Values Activities for Refugees and Children-Affected-by-War?

_____

_____

_____

_____

Evaluation Form
Educator Training Workshops

Which sessions did you benefit most from? _____

_____

_____

_____

What contributed to that? _____

_____

_____

_____

Were there any sessions you did not benefit from? _____

_____

_____

_____

What contributed to that? _____

_____

_____

_____

What did you enjoy the most? _____

_____

_____

_____

Training Components

Please rate the following:

	Poor	Fair	Good	Excellent
The overall program				
Content				
Process				
Quality of interactions				

Any suggestions? Is there anything else you would like us to know?

_____

_____

_____

_____

Name (optional) _____

THANK YOU

Evaluation Form for Parents Participating in Living Values Parent Groups

What did you benefit from learning in the Living Values Parent Group sessions?_____

_____

_____

_____

_____

How do you think this will help your child? (Or, what changes have you seen?) _____

_____

_____

_____

_____

Was anything not of benefit? _____

_____

_____

_____

_____

What did you enjoy the most? _____

_____

_____

_____

_____

Training Components

Please rate the following:

	Poor	Fair	Good	Excellent
The overall program				
Content				
Process				
Quality of interactions				

Any suggestions? Is there anything else you would like us to know?

_____

_____

_____

_____

Name (optional) _____

THANK YOU

Optional Student Evaluation Form 1

What are your favorite values? Why? _____

_____

_____

_____

_____

What have you learned? _____

_____

_____

_____

_____

What would you like to do more of? _____

_____

_____

_____

_____

Please check the box to the right that best fits the statement.

	Much More	A little More	The same	Not at all
I understand the value of peace				
I think I have more respect for myself				
I have more respect for others				
I can communicate better when there is a conflict				

Training Components

(continued)	Much More	A little More	The same	Not at all
I can concentrate better				
I think I know myself better				
I give more happiness to others				
I know how to cooperate				
I feel I can contribute to a better world				
I enjoy being at school more				

Any suggestions? Is there anything else you would like us to know? Is there anything you need?

_____

_____

_____

_____

Name (optional) _____ Date: _____

THANK YOU

Training Components

Optional Student Evaluation Form 2

Name: _____   Date: _____

List of identified values	In which situations?	The most important ones. Why?

Optional Student Evaluation Form 3

Name: _____   Date: _____

The value I have discovered	Situations in which it is useful	When I recognize it: always, sometimes, never

Training Components

9. USING THE EDUCATOR TRAINING GUIDE

A short session to introduce this LVEP Educator Training Guide can be held near the beginning or near the end of the Train-the-Trainer seminar.

Inform TTT participants about the organization of the LVEP Educator Training Guide. The "Using the Educator Training Guide" section at the beginning of this book describes what is in each chapter, and the Training Components overhead (available in chapter III) shows how the Training Components are organized. Near the end of the TTT, participants will have been through many of the sessions within this manual.

The overhead masters are available in color on the Living Values Web site at *www.livingvalues.net.*

Provide copies if they do not already have one, and answer any questions.

Training Components

10. ADULT PRESENTATION SKILLS (TTTs ONLY)

Introductory Remarks

"Most educators work with children or young adults the majority of the time. Some of you are (or may be) teacher trainers and are accustomed to switching teaching styles. When conducting an LVEP training, it is important to meet adult learning needs. As mentioned on page four of this manual, it is recommended that everyone attending the TTT already have some skills in training adults or facilitating groups. Sometimes, however, people attend the TTT because of their enthusiasm and love for the program. Some are not accustomed to facilitating or presenting to adult groups. Hence, this section is intended as a review for some and needed guidance for others.

"Think for a moment about how you like to learn new information and skills. This list (put up an overhead or note the points on a flipchart) notes characteristics that adult learners share."

Adult learners are:

- Goal oriented
- Influenced by past learning experiences

Training Components

- Have ingrained habits
- Interested by being actively involved
- Relate what they're learning to what they already know
- Motivated to learn when the material appears relevant

Ask:

- Are there others that you can think of? (Add these to the list either on the flipchart or on the overhead.)
- What are the implications for the way you conduct a Living Values Educator Training?

Their answers may include:

- Be clear about the training objectives
- Know who is coming and how they want to use the materials
- Have sessions that mix lecture with group discussions
- Be able to generate case studies and examples relevant to their audience, etc.

The LVEP Trainer Plays Many Roles

"As a trainer or facilitator of a LVEP Educator Training or a TTT, you are responsible for creating an atmosphere that ensures a positive learning experience for the participants. Since the training you are conducting is about values-based learning, you will want to create an environment that is warm, caring, full of regard for each participant and fun.

"The trainer may be part of an LVEP Planning Team. The trainer will need to know the material and have meetings with other presenters, key people, coaches, and individuals helping with logistics to determine roles and responsibilities. Some of the roles of the Lead Trainer could be Meeting Planner, Group Facilitator, Trainer and Coach. Leading the sessions requires preparation and a thorough knowledge of the content. One person could play all the roles in a small training. In large trainings or in a TTT there may be two or three individuals who play the role of a trainer/facilitator as well as additional coaches. It is important to know the skills of the presentation team. The trainers should prepare a working agenda with the requesting institution(s) and be equipped to help the process flow smoothly as well as evaluate the results."

The Trainer as an Effective Meeting Planner

The trainer will need to be an effective meeting planner. Some suggested responsibilities and behaviors for the trainer and/or LVEP Planning Team include:

- Conduct a needs assessment with the requesting institute(s) to plan an appropriate agenda with relevant training components.
- Prepare the site for a welcoming learning experience.
- Communicate objectives to the participants prior to the training.
- Have materials prepared to hand out to participants, including an agenda and LVEP materials.
- Welcome participants as they arrive.
- Arrange for any special equipment needed during the sessions.

The Trainer as an Effective Group Facilitator

Some suggested responsibilities and behaviors of an effective group facilitator include:

- Review aims of the session with participants.
- Make use of a variety of learning tools such as lectures, imagery, small group discussions and eliciting feedback. (A variety is used within the training component sessions.)
- Be able to generate appropriate examples for the group.
- Respect and support each person.
- Observe group energy and other nonverbal clues and make adjustments.
- When asking questions, use open-ended questions.
- Allow space, silence, and time for participants to reflect and respond.
- Ask questions or give examples to keep interest level up and to check for understanding, pace, involvement and relevancy.
- Listen.
- If you do not know the answers, be honest and say so. Then find the answer and report back.
- Trust the process, and stay positive and clear.
- Have a sense of humor.
- Be yourself.

In addition to excellent facilitation skills, a trainer will need adult presentation skills for large groups. Some suggested responsibilities and behaviors for an LVEP trainer include:

- Communicate and contract with the group about time and participation. (See Ground Rules at the end of Training Component I, Chapter II.)
- Excellent presentation skills for large group sessions.
- A thorough knowledge of LVEP history, partners and structure.
- Thorough knowledge of any didactic material presented in lectures. Find someone else to present that information if you are not comfortable.
- Check with the large group periodically to ask for questions, concerns and any needs. They may be interested in "working groups" or other topics.

Training Components

- Partner with teacher trainers in identifying any resources needed to implement teacher training.
- Work with teacher trainers to plan effective training and ongoing support.
- Ask participants to evaluate the training and review results with team members.

And a Coach

Some suggested responsibilities and behaviors of an effective coach, in addition to facilitation skills, include:

- Plan values activities with participants using Living Values activities from two values units.
- In your values activities session with the participants, use a variety of activities.
- Help participants after the session in their commitments and strategies for teacher training.
- Review evaluations from teacher training and support ongoing work of teachers and trainers.

Recommendation

If the participant attending the TTT has not taken any LVEP seminars prior, it is recommended that he or she enjoy teaching the activities and implementing strategies prior to conducting a training.

A Final Thought for TTTs

When you hear something, you forget it.

When you see something, you remember it.

But not until you do something will you understand it.

11. GOALS AND IMPLEMENTATION STRATEGIES

Session One: Goals and Implementation Strategies

The trainer(s) will need to plan this session with the participating educational institution(s) prior to the training. Factors to consider during your planning session are:

Time Required

When doing training with cooperating partners, or different school districts widely separated by miles within a country, there may be a need to allow several hours of planning time during the LVEP workshop. In other trainings participants may wish only a brief time for planning. This may be because they are in the same area and can engage in a detailed planning process once the training is completed.

Who Should Be in Each Planning Team?

Teams can be formed according to:

- Area—school, district, country or region
- Role—primary teachers, secondary teachers, teachers, principals/head teachers, core values education teachers, teacher trainers, ministry officials, university lecturers, representatives from several cooperating institutions

When Is It Best to Begin the Planning Process During the Training?

If several hours are included for planning within the training, it works well to include a brief session on goals after the Rekindling the Dream session of Training Component 2. This can be done informally, asking participants to discuss tentative goals in small groups, or simply asking what they want for their students.

Usually a planning session toward the end of the training works well. Please see the sample agendas.

Planning Questions for Each Group

- What are our goals?
- What do we need to achieve those goals?
- What are the likely obstacles?
- Make an action plan, detailing goals and implementation strategies. Include a timeline and responsibilities.

The trainer may wish to briefly talk about any perceived "needs." For example, it is important that each area include songs and stories from their own culture(s). A team of teachers for the district or country may wish to do that at the primary level, with another team doing the same at the secondary level. Translation may be another need.

A Thorough Plan

Another option is for school site teams to be given the opportunity to apply the skills they have learned by filling out the theoretical model in relation to their educational site. Ask them to identify the pluses and minuses, and identify their school ethos. Then make a plan to increase the pluses and deal with the minuses. Afterwards, write the implementation strategies down in an action plan, specifying timelines and responsible people.

Session Two: A Blueprint:

How to Introduce a Values-Based Curriculum

Some schools want additional information on how to work with their school staff when introducing a values education program. A blueprint is offered below by Neil Hawkes, a headteacher at the West Kidlington Primary School in Oxford, England.

1. Rationale

Decide why you want to have a policy to introduce a values-based curriculum. Consider issues such as pressures which society places on children as they are growing up, e.g., constantly being bombarded with materialism. Consider issues related to the context of your own school, such as the aims of the school and the range of children that it serves.

• Be clear about the core values that you wish to introduce into the school.

Study *Living Values: A Guidebook* and *LVEP's Living Values Activities* and decide how the core values should be integrated into school life.

- Remember that the way you introduce values into your school will be dependent on your particular context and the needs of your pupils.

2. Method

- Create a whole school climate where values are seen as vital in underpinning the curriculum. Talk about your school ethos, and look at the ways that you do things in your school. Consider relationships, behavior and attitudes. Think about how your school contributes to the spiritual, moral, social and cultural development of your pupils. Identify subjects which make specific contributions, and consider any particular methods that you currently use that promote the values of the school.
- In order to create a positive school climate, there must be a commitment by the whole staff: that values-based education is central to the school's mission. Throughout the process of introducing core values there must be staff, pupil, family and community involvement.

Key Teachers

Identify key teachers who can act as primary facilitators. These teachers, through their enthusiasm, commitment and "walking their talk," create the impetus which ensures that values lie at the core of the curriculum.

Give time for key teachers to analyze the current ethos of the school by determining the elements of good practices that already exist. Celebrating current good practices is key to encouraging teachers to develop values-based education.

Once good practice areas are identified, they can be built on and extended by referring to LVEP and other resources which support values-based education programs.

What Are the Needs of Children?

Next, look at the needs of the children in your school. Consider how students learn best, and also discuss how teachers can model the values they wish to impart through their own behavior and expectations.

How Do We Meet These Needs?

Match the teaching methods and content of the curriculum to the needs of the children as identified above. Also, look for cross-curricular links which will enable pupils to recognize that values underpin all subject areas.

Skills We Wish to Develop

Consider the skills that you want the pupils to develop which contribute to reflective thinking about values.

Activities to Develop These Skills

Identify learning activities that support values-based education, and look for appropriate resources.

Benefits for Pupils

Identify the benefits that pupils will experience as values-based education is introduced. Issues concerning standards, quality of learning, increasing self-esteem and the development of reflective practices, should all be considered.

Conclusion

It is vitally important that all staff members feel involved in the process, so consideration must be given to in-service education. Throughout the process, share the development with parents and the wider school community.

Finally, ensure that the process is well-planned, monitored and evaluated in order to keep the process alive and constantly under review.

Writing a policy based on the school's practice makes a public statement about the school's commitment to values education. This policy can be discussed with new members of staff and the community in general. It helps to ensure consistency of approach throughout the school.

Below is an example of West Kidlington School's policy, which should be read in the context of British education.

West Kidlington Primary and Nursery Schools Values Education Policy

Aim:

To raise standards by promoting a school ethos which is underpinned by core values that support the development of the whole child as a reflective learner.

Rationale:

At West Kidlington we are giving a great deal of thought to the values that we are trying to promote in school. We regularly consider our core values and how the school sustains an ethos which supports the pupil as a reflective learner and promotes quality teaching and learning. We are very aware that society is faced with enormously complicated problems which makes growing up a very difficult process. Children are constantly bombarded with negative messages which adversely affect their mental, emotional and spiritual development. Also, they are repeatedly being given the impression that happiness is totally obtainable from a material world. They are conditioned to believe that "things" will provide happiness. For example, advertisements encourage children to believe that the only source of entertainment is derived from the television or video! They are generally encouraged to experience life in a world totally external to their innerselves: a world which is full of noise and constant activity. Impressions of society being violent and selfish leave their mark as the child develops into adolescence. Symptoms of pupil stress are seen as children find it difficult to listen attentively and to give schoolwork their full concentration. Social relationships suffer as the child often fails to appreciate that building meaningful relationships is their responsibility.

As a school community, we believe the ethos of the school should be built on a foundation of core values such as honesty, respect, happiness, responsibility, tolerance and peace. These will at times be addressed directly through lessons and the acts of worship program, while at others they will permeate the whole curriculum. Either way, they are the basis for the social, intellectual, emotional, spiritual and moral development of the whole child. We encourage pupils to consider these values, thereby developing knowledge, skills and attitudes which enable them to develop as reflective learners and grow to be stable, educated and civil adults.

Elements of Teaching and Learning

The elements of values education are:

- Ensuring that the school's institutional values are consistent with the values that the pupils are encouraged to develop.

- By actively promoting a whole school policy that has the support of all staff and is led and monitored by the headteacher.
- Through a program of school assemblies that introduce the monthly values, pupils are encouraged to be involved in exploring their understanding of values in pupil-led assemblies.
- By direct teaching about values in values lessons. These lessons provide opportunities for personal reflection, moral discourse and an appropriate activity to promote understanding. Teaching and learning about values takes place in the following steps:
    1. By teachers explaining the meaning of a value.
    2. By pupils reflecting on the value and relating it to their own behavior.
    3. By pupils using the value to guide their own actions.
- By staff modeling the values through their own behavior.
- By ensuring that values are taught implicitly through every aspect of the curriculum.
- Through the work of the pupils' school council.
- By involving all staff, governors and parents in the values program. This is done through newsletters and meetings explaining how home and school can work together to promote positive values.

Resources

Lesson plans and library resources which the school has developed.

The lesson plans of the Human Values Foundation.

Materials from Living Values: An Educational Program. This program is supported by

UNESCO, sponsored by the Brahma Kumaris, and in consultation with the Education Cluster of UNICEF (New York).

Training Components

12. CLOSING SESSION

The Closing Session Can Include Several Elements:

- Teams report back to the Plenary Session—Values Activities Teams and/or Planning Teams can report. Allocate time for each group.
- Sharing songs or talents—Some groups have enjoyed sharing skits, sketches, music, poetry and dance.
- Sharing of experiences—Some LVEP trainings have ended with the entire group sitting in a large circle, each person sharing one sentence about what they enjoyed most or learned. In other trainings, several people have shared, or the leading representative of the institute or a Minister of Education has shared insights.
- Present an LVEP Certificate to each participant.

CHAPTER III:

Handouts and Overhead Masters

$\mathscr{L}$IVING $\mathscr{V}$ALUES: AN EDUCATIONAL PROGRAM

Abstract

April 2000

The Call for Values

The call for values is currently echoing around the globe, as educators, parents and more and more children are increasingly concerned about and affected by violence, growing social problems, and the lack of respect for each other and the world around them. Therefore, society is once again asking educators to address these problems. As UNESCO's Commission on Education for the Twenty-First Century, headed by Jacques Delors, reports in *Learning: The Treasure Within*[1], "In confronting the many challenges that the future holds in store, humankind sees in education an indispensable asset in its attempt to attain the ideals of peace, freedom and social justice. The Commission does not see education as a miracle cure or a magic formula opening the door to a world in which all ideals will be attained, but as one of the principle means available to foster a deeper and more harmonious form of human development and thereby to reduce poverty, exclusion, ignorance, oppression and war." *Living Values: An Educational Program* (LVEP) has been produced in response to the call for values.

---

1. Delors, Jacques, et al. *Learning: The Treasure Within,* Report to UNESCO of the International Commission on Education for the Twenty-first Century. UNESCO Publishing, 1996. ISBN 0 7306 9037 7

What Kind of Program Is LVEP?

Living Values: An Educational Program is a values education program. It offers a variety of experiential values activities and practical methodologies to teachers and facilitators to enable children and young adults to explore and develop twelve key universal values: Cooperation, Freedom, Happiness, Honesty, Humility, Love, Peace, Respect, Responsibility, Simplicity, Tolerance and Unity. LVEP also has special materials for use with parents and caregivers, and children affected-by-war.

The purpose of *Living Values: An Educational Program* is to provide guiding principles and tools for the development of the whole person, recognizing that the individual is comprised of physical, intellectual, emotional and spiritual dimensions.

The aims are:

- To help individuals think about and reflect on different values and the practical implications of expressing them in relation to themselves, others, the community and the world at large;
- To deepen understanding, motivation and responsibility with regard to making positive personal and social choices;
- To inspire individuals to choose their own personal, social, moral and spiritual values and be aware of practical methods for developing and deepening them; and
- To encourage educators and caregivers to look at education as providing students with a philosophy of living, thereby facilitating their overall growth, development and choices so they may integrate themselves into the community with respect, confidence and purpose.

Current Status

Living Values: An Educational Program is a partnership among educators around the world. It is currently supported by UNESCO, sponsored by the Spanish Committee of UNICEF, the Planet Society and the Brahma Kumaris, in consultation with the Education Cluster of UNICEF (New York).

Living Values: An Educational Program, Inc. is registered as a nonprofit organization in the USA. The LVEP International Coordinating Office is in New York. Many countries involved in LVEP have formed national associations, usually comprised of educators, education officials and representatives of organizations involved with education.

The Living Values Educators' Kit became available for piloting in March 1997, and by late spring that year was being piloted at 220 sites in over forty countries. By April 2000, LVEP was in use at over 1,800 sites in sixty-four countries.

Materials

In 1999, the *Living Values Educators' Kit* began to be divided into six books and expanded with contributions from educators around the world. The current six LVEP books are:

- *Living Values Activities for Children Ages 3–7*
- *Living Values Activities for Children Ages 8–14*
- *Living Values Activities for Young Adults*
- *LVEP Educator Training Guide*
- *Living Values for Parent Groups: A Facilitator Guide*
- *Living Values Activities for Refugees and Children-Affected-by-War*

- In the *Living Values Activities for Children Ages 3–7, Ages 8–14,* and *Living Values Activities for Young Adults,* reflective and imaging activities encourage students to access their own creativity and inner gifts. Communication activities teach students to implement peaceful social skills. Artistic activities, songs and dance inspire students to express themselves while experiencing the value of focus. Game-like activities are thought-provoking and fun; the discussion time that follows those activities helps students explore effects of different attitudes and behaviors. Other activities stimulate awareness of personal and social responsibility and, for older students, awareness of social justice. The development of self-esteem and tolerance continues throughout the exercises. Educators are encouraged to utilize their own rich heritage while integrating values into everyday activities and the curriculum. Please see the goals in each Living Value Activities book for more specific information.

- *LVEP Educator Training Guide*—This guide contains the variety of workshops found within LVEP Educator Trainings. Sessions include values awareness, creating a values-based atmosphere, and skills for creating such an atmosphere. Sample training agendas are offered for one-, two-, and three-day educator training programs and a five-day train-the-trainer session.

- *Living Values Parent Groups: A Facilitator Guide*—These facilitated sessions are designed for parents and caregivers to develop the understanding and skills needed to encourage and positively develop values in children. The process includes sessions which help parents reflect on their own values and how they "live" those values. In many group sessions, parents play the games their children will play and learn additional methods to foster values-related social and emotional skills at home. Common parenting concerns are addressed, as are particular skills to deal with those concerns.

Handouts and Overhead Masters

- *Living Values Activities for Refugees and Children-Affected-by-War*—This unique series of activities gives children an opportunity to begin the healing process while learning about peace. Sixty daily lessons provide tools to release and deal with grief while developing positive adaptive social and emotional skills with the values of peace, respect and love. Teachers are encouraged to do the regular values activities after the lessons are completed.
- Living Values Card Pack—Inspired by *Living Values: A Guidebook,* these forty-eight cards are designed as a tool for teachers and students to explore inner values—through reflection, discussion, an activity and practice. Designed by Casa Productions.

LVEP materials have been translated into many languages. The *Living Values Educators' Kit* is available in English, French and Spanish. The current set of six books is available in English. Translation is ongoing in Arabic, Chinese, German, Greek, Hebrew, Hindi, Hungarian, Italian, Japanese, Karen, Malay, Polish, Portuguese, Russian, Spanish, Thai, Turkish and Vietnamese.

Background

Living Values: An Educational Program grew out of an international project begun in 1995 by the Brahma Kumaris to celebrate the fiftieth anniversary of the United Nations. Called Sharing Our Values for a Better World, this project focused on twelve universal values. The theme—adopted from a tenet in the Preamble of the United Nations' Charter—was "To reaffirm faith in fundamental human rights, in the dignity and worth of the human person. . . ."

Living Values: A Guidebook was created as part of the Sharing Our Values for a Better World Project. The guidebook—which provided value statements on the twelve core values, offered an individual perspective for creating and sustaining positive change, and included facilitated group workshops and activities—contained a small section of values activities for students in the classroom. That sketchy classroom curriculum became the inspiration and impetus for Living Values: An Educational Initiative (LVEI).

Living Values: An Educational Initiative (LVEI) was born when twenty educators from around the world gathered at UNICEF Headquarters in New York City in August of 1996 to discuss the needs of children, their experiences of working with values and how educators can integrate values to better prepare students for lifelong learning. Using *Living Values: A Guidebook* and the "Convention on the Rights of the Child" as a framework, the global educators identified and agreed upon the purpose and aims of values-based education worldwide—in both developed and developing countries. Living Values Education has been gaining momentum since.

Living Values Web site
www.livingvalues.net

*L*IVING *V*ALUES: AN EDUCATIONAL PROGRAM

Results

Living Values: An Educational Program is a values education program. It offers a variety of experiential values activities and practical methodologies to teachers and facilitators to enable children and young adults to explore and develop twelve key universal values: Cooperation, Freedom, Happiness, Honesty, Humility, Love, Peace, Respect, Responsibility, Simplicity, Tolerance and Unity. LVEP also has special materials for use with parents and caregivers, and children-affected-by-war.

The purpose of *Living Values: An Educational Program* is to provide guiding principles and tools for the development of the whole person, recognizing that the individual is comprised of physical, intellectual, emotional and spiritual dimensions.

Pilot Results—June 1998

Initial pilot results from schools indicate increased motivation in students, more cooperative and respectful behaviors with both peers and teachers, and more ability to focus on school tasks. While most sites began their pilot in the spring of 1997, a few schools had been experimenting since 1995 with Living Values activities from the Sharing Our Values for a Better World Classroom Curriculum in *Living Values: A Guidebook.*

West Kidlington Primary School in Oxford, England, began Living Values classroom activities in 1995. The headteacher, in this working-class neighborhood school Mr. Neil Hawkes, reported that students learned to be responsible for their behavior. He noted: "They enjoy peaceful, respectful, cooperative relationships with their peers and teachers. The school enables the students to think carefully about values and to reflect values in their behavior and attitudes. School assemblies have become a powerful vehicle for teaching values, raising self-esteem and developing enthusiasm." The school recently won recognition for its outstanding work in the areas of moral, social and cultural education. Parents voice appreciation for the changes and are involved in the values education process as relevant assignments are brought home for discussion. Mr. Hawkes is of the opinion that when an entire school focuses on values, the impact is greater and more positive.

Mr. Peter Williams worked with somewhat older students for several months in a middle school in Beijing, China. When he asked his Chinese colleague, Ms. Ao Wen Ya, why she thought a peace imagining exercise was successful, she said: "It helped the children to find peace by themselves. It helped the children to feel happy and relaxed. It made them really want to be happy and motivated to build a better world and be kind to each other." She additionally noted, "Sometimes the children can be naughty in class; they don't concentrate. Now they are more engaged in their subjects because they are interested. They are motivated to learn because they are valued as people. . . . They are now calmer and not as naughty. The quality and standards of work are higher. They are willing to take risks to express themselves well with more confidence." Mr. Williams added, "The lessons really did something. Their attitude is more positive, and they are better organized both individually and as a group." An observer from the Chinese Academy of Sciences commented that the motivation of the children had been greatly enhanced, and it transferred to other lessons.

In Zimbabwe, Ms. Natasha Ncube used Living Values Educational materials with her class at Prince Edward Boys' High School in Harare. She felt the reflection activities helped improve discipline; the storytelling and discussions allowed her to learn individual opinions of the students; and the group work developed unity, cooperation, patience and tolerance in students. Her comments: "Discipline has improved. I noticed the development of self-confidence in many students, appreciation, recognition of values in others, as well as in the self. The students became more open-minded, not only confident, and also fearless in expression of their own opinion." She also noted that many students began doing their work on time because they had developed more conscientiousness: "They believed in themselves." She noted some did their work before because of fear of academic detention or corporal punishment.

In La Paz, Bolivia, three thousand students from three to eighteen years in age engaged in Living Values activities at the German School. Cecilia Levy noted that discriminatory behavior has decreased, and unity has grown. She stated, "Students have become more positive in every way—in their tone of voice and manner when they interact with others. The teachers involved have noted changes in their own attitudes and how that affects the atmosphere in the classroom." One hundred and twenty parents took part in the parent values classes. The parents felt the classes were very beneficial. An unexpected result was more understanding and cooperation between parents and teachers.

Program Results—June 1999

In teacher program evaluations of June 1999, teachers from South Africa noted positive growth in their students in the areas of self-confidence, showing respect for adults and honesty. Ms. Geswindt, a middle school teacher, also noted that her students improved in taking responsibility and the ability to resolve conflicts and cooperate, and showed more respect for their peers. A preschool teacher in Mombassa, Kenya, noted that 90 percent of her students demonstrated improvement in overall school functioning and highlighted positive changes in all areas in which values were taught.

Handouts and Overhead Masters

Twenty-seven teachers in Malaysia consistently noted good results even though the program has been implemented only for a short time. One secondary teacher said, "I was surprised that through this program my students learned to understand more about their feelings toward others." Mr. Mohdsura noted positive growth in motivation, respect toward peers and adults, honesty, responsibility and the ability to cooperate. The teachers who evaluated the program noticed positive changes in the students and in the classroom atmosphere as a whole. The Malaysian report noted: "What was once regarded as a dreaded subject, was now looked forward to, so that they could share their thoughts, feelings and ideas with others. Many teachers reported that students were more confident, more aware of the effect of actions on others, more respectful of others' feelings, and overall were just happier and more self-assured."

A teacher in England for nine- to eleven-year-old students, Ms. Davidson, noted: "My heart was constantly touched by the children's enthusiasm and desire for Living Values work. I was constantly amazed by the absolute beauty of the children's work and the silence they worked in."

Refugee teachers at two camps in Thailand have been using LVEP's Living Values Activities for Refugees and Children-Affected-by-War. The educators noted that it is the favorite class of the day for students, and that the students are more expressive and "well mannered." The sadness and anger exhibited by some of the students is noticeably diminished. The director of the two camps has requested training for all the teachers.

In Mauritius, educator Mrs. Nellapotesawmy noted, "Pupils are more honest. They share their knowledge with friends in difficulty. Quarrels are less frequent, for they are learning to respect and love their friends." Mr. Borthosow added, "The values do help a lot to give satisfaction to one and all. Frankly, the complaints like 'Monsieur, he hit me,' 'He pushed me,' 'He took my cake,'

'He doesn't allow me to play,' have diminished a lot."

LVEP Train-the-Trainer programs and LVEP Educator trainings are increasing around the world. There has been considerable cooperation between Spain and Latin America. In July 1999, a European forum, Living Our Values: The Spirit of Education for the Twenty-First Century was held in Barcelona, Spain. While a high-level dialogue was enjoyed by participants from all over Europe, the highlight was the arrival of a boatload of children from France who did Living Values activities on the way.

Note: While all evaluations completed by educators about the results of using LVEP materials have been positive, there are evaluations from a limited number of sites. Newcastle University in Australia is beginning a more formal evaluation of results at seven schools which recently began implementing the program. Several other regions are considering independent evaluations.

Living Values Web site

www.livingvalues.net

Ice-Breaker Bingo

I would like to swim with dolphins.	I like to play children's games.	I remember to say please, thank you and excuse me.	Values help me make decisions.	If I were a flower, I would be a rose.
I play two or more musical instruments.	I value simplicity, simplicity, simplicity!	I love to dance!	I speak three or more languages.	I feel peaceful when I garden.
I whistle while I work.	I like to travel.	FREE	I love chocolate ice cream.	I have taken one minute of courage to tell the truth.
I have been a teacher for more than twenty years.	I admire Martin Luther King Jr.	Patience is my greatest asset.	One of the values I believe in most is love.	I feel inner freedom when I _____.
I believe in giving and taking happiness.	I like to listen to children.	I did not cooperate once.	My favorite subject in school was math.	Teaching is my life!

*L*IVING *V*ALUES: AN EDUCATIONAL PROGRAM
Educator Reporting Form

Date: _____

Educator's Name: _____ Position: _____

Educator's School/Organization: _____

School Address: _____ City:_____

Country: _____ Phone/Fax/E-mail:_____

Month and Year You Started Using LVEP: _____

Please circle the edition you are using: Living Values Educators' Kit or *Living Values Activities* books

Who

What were the ages of the students you did LVEP activities with? _____

How many students participated? _____

How many educators were involved at your site? _____ Out of how many? _____

Did the entire school participate in a values program? Please circle: Yes or No

Values of Focus

Please circle the values you have focused on in the classroom/school.

Peace	Respect	Love	Cooperation	Freedom	Happiness
Honesty	Humility	Responsibility	Simplicity	Tolerance	Unity

Did you use SOME, MOST or ALL of the LVEP activities in the units you did? (Circle one)

Did you incorporate values into the curriculum? _____

When

Values Activities, including incorporating values into the curriculum, were done:

Circle one:	5-20 min.	21-40 min.	41-60 min.	More than 1 hour	Most of day
Circle one:	Once a month	Once a week	Twice a week	Three times a week	Daily

What percentage of the time do you feel there is a values-based atmosphere? ____%

Handouts and Overhead Masters

Results

Please tell us about any changes you have observed in the students that might be attributed to their experiences in this program. Kindly approximate changes in the chart below, or describe changes. Please write in the percentage of students for which this is applicable.

90% of the students or ____% of the students	Good growth	A little better	The same	A little worse	Much worse
Self-confidence	5	4	3	2	1
Respect toward peers	5	4	3	2	1
Respect toward adults	5	4	3	2	1
Ability to resolve conflicts	5	4	3	2	1
Ability to cooperate	5	4	3	2	1
Responsibility	5	4	3	2	1
Honesty	5	4	3	2	1
Ability to focus/concentrate	5	4	3	2	1
Social skills	5	4	3	2	1
Interest in school/motivation	5	4	3	2	1
Overall school functioning	5	4	3	2	1

Please share any personal changes you experienced as a result of doing the program.

_____

_____

_____

_____

Is there anything else you would like us to know?

_____

_____

_____

_____

We would appreciate you sharing a "Success Story" below. Or, would you like to write one on the LVEP Web site? The address is *http://www.livingvalues.net*

_____

_____

_____

_____

Your students can put their pictures, poems, projects, etc. up on the Web site, too.

_____

_____

_____

_____

THANK YOU

Quantitative Report
For LVEP Country Coordinators

Date: _____

Name of Coordinator: _____ Country: _____

Coordinator's Address: _____

Coordinator's Phone/Fax/E-mail: _____

Dates of Pilot Started: _____ To: _____

Teacher Training

Please tell us about any LVEP Educator Trainings in your country. You may wish to include if it was a one-, two- or three-day training, and the number of teachers involved.

_____

_____

_____

_____

_____

What is the relationship with your country's Ministry of Education or other organizations?

_____

_____

_____

_____

_____

Schools

How many sites/schools were involved doing LVEP Values Activities? Was the entire school involved at those sites, or one or two teachers? If you can, please indicate which cities or states the schools are in.

_____ Day Care Centers/Nursery Schools

_____ Elementary Schools

_____ Middle Schools

_____ High Schools/Secondary Schools

_____ Other organizations

Parent Values Groups

Please let us know if there have been or are Living Values Parent Groups, or if you are using the materials in other ways.

_____

_____

_____

_____

Any other thoughts? Anything else we should know? Did you use the Living Values Activities for Refugees and Children-Affected-by-War?

_____

_____

_____

_____

Evaluation Form
Educator Training Workshops

Which sessions did you benefit most from? _____

_____

_____

_____

What contributed to that? _____

_____

_____

_____

Were there any sessions you did not benefit from? _____

_____

_____

_____

What contributed to that? _____

_____

_____

_____

What did you enjoy the most? _____

_____

_____

_____

Please rate the following:

	Poor	Fair	Good	Excellent
The overall program				
Content				
Process				
Quality of interactions				

Any suggestions? Is there anything else you would like us to know?

_____

_____

_____

_____

Name (optional) _____

THANK YOU

Evaluation Form for Parents Participating in the Living Values Parent Group

What did you benefit from learning in the Living Values Parent Group sessions? _____

_____

_____

_____

_____

How do you think this will help your child? (Or, what changes have you seen?) ____

_____

_____

_____

_____

_____

Was anything not of benefit? _____

_____

_____

_____

_____

What did you enjoy the most? _____

_____

_____

_____

_____

Please rate the following:

	Poor	Fair	Good	Excellent
The overall program				
Content				
Process				
Quality of interactions				

Any suggestions? Is there anything else you would like us to know?

_____

_____

_____

_____

Name (optional) _____

THANK YOU

Optional Student Evaluation Form 1

What are your favorite values? Why? _____

_____

_____

_____

_____

What have you learned? _____

_____

_____

_____

_____

What would you like to do more of? _____

_____

_____

_____

_____

Please check the box to the right that best fits the statement.

	Much More	A little More	The same	Not at all
I understand the value of peace				
I think I have more respect for myself				
I have more respect for others				
I can communicate better when there is a conflict				

(continued)	Much More	A little More	The same	Not at all
I can concentrate better				
I think I know myself better				
I give more happiness to others				
I know how to cooperate				
I feel I can contribute to a better world				
I enjoy being at school more				

Any suggestions? Is there anything else you would like us to know? Is there anything you need?

_____

_____

_____

_____

Name (optional) _____ Date: _____

THANK YOU

Handouts and Overhead Masters

Optional Student Evaluation Form 2

Name: _____   Date: _____

List of identified values	In which situations?	The most important ones. Why?

Optional Student Evaluation Form 3

Name: _____   Date: _____

The value I have discovered	Situations in which it is useful	When I recognize it: always, sometimes, never . . .

The United Nations Convention on the Rights of the Child

Article 29

1. States Parties agree that the education of the child shall be directed to:

a) The development of the child's personality, talents and mental and physical abilities to their fullest potential;

b) The development of respect for human rights and fundamental freedoms, and for the principles enshrined in the Charter of the United Nations;

c) The development of respect for the child's parents, his or her own cultural identity, language and values, for the national values of the country in which the child is living, the country from which he or she may originate, and for civilizations different from his or her own;

d) The preparation of the child for responsible life in a free society, in the spirit of understanding, peace, tolerance, equality of sexes, and friendship among all peoples, ethnic, national and religious groups and persons of indigenous origin;

e) The development of respect for the natural environment.

Howard Gardener's Multiple Intelligences

- The **Body/Kinesthetic**

- The **Environmental/Ethical**

- The **Logical/Mathematical**

- The **Musical/Rhythmic**

- The **Interpersonal**

- The **Intrapersonal**

- The **Verbal/Linguistic**

- The **Visual/Spatial**

*L*iving *V*alues:
An Educational Program

Exploring and developing
universal values for a better world

*

Peace   Respect   Love

Happiness   Freedom

Honesty   Humility

Tolerance   Cooperation

Responsibility   Simplicity

Unity

*L*IVING *V*ALUES:
An Educational Program

Is a partnership among educators around the world

Supported by UNESCO

Sponsored by

- Spanish National Committee of UNICEF

- Planet Society

- Brahma Kumaris

In consultation with the Education Cluster
of UNICEF (New York)

_L_IVING _V_ALUES:
An Educational Program

Purpose

To provide guiding principles
and tools for development
of the whole person,
recognizing that the individual
is comprised of physical,
intellectual, emotional,
and spiritual dimensions.

*L*IVING *V*ALUES:
An Educational Program

Aims

- To help individuals think about and reflect on different values and the practical implications of expressing them in relation to themselves, others, the community and the world at large;

- To deepen understanding, motivation, and responsibility with regard to making positive personal and social choices;

- To inspire individuals to choose their own personal, social, moral, and spiritual values and be aware of practical methods for developing and deepening them; and

- To encourage educators and caregivers to look at education as providing students with a philosophy of living, thereby facilitating their overall growth, development, and choices so they may integrate themselves into the community with respect, confidence, and purpose.

*L*iving *V*alues:
An Educational Program

Sharing Our Values for a Better World

An international project to celebrate the

50th anniversary of the United Nations

The theme of Living Values

was adopted from a tenet in the

Preamble of the United

Nations Charter.

"To reaffirm faith in fundamental

human rights, in the dignity and worth

of the human person. . . ."

LIVING VALUES:
An Educational Program

"Its birth"

Living Values: A Guidebook

- Education Cluster of UNICEF (New York)

- Twenty educators representing five continents met in New York at UNICEF Headquarters in August 1996

- Convention on the Rights of the Child

*L*iving *V*alues:
An Educational Program

Living Values Educators' Kit
February 1997

Contains 12 sections:

1. Setting the Context
2. Commitment
3. Educators' Manual
4. Blueprint: Values Based Curriculum
5. Values Activities for Children 2–7
6. Values Activities for Children 8–14
7. Values Activities for Young Adults
8. Parents/Caregivers Module
9. Appendix for Values Activities
10. Evaluations
11. Train the Trainers
12. Refugees Module

*L*IVING *V*ALUES:
An Educational Program

Six LVEP Books

Developed in 1999 and the early part of 2000

Living Values Activities for Children Ages 3–7

Living Values Activities for Children Ages 8–14

Living Values Activities for Young Adults

Living Values Parent Groups: A Facilitator Guide

Living Values Activities for Refugees and Children-
Affected-by-War

LVEP Educator Training Guide

$\mathscr{L}$IVING $\mathscr{V}$ALUES:
An Educational Program

Where We Are Now

LVEP
- Is in use in 64 Countries
- At more than 1,800 Sites
- Translating continues

Global and Regional TTT Sessions
- Train-the-Trainer for Educators
- Training Facilitators for LVEP Parent Values Groups

Countries and Regions
- LVEP Educator Training

In Countries with Refugee Camps
- Training educators to use Living Values
- Activities for Refugees and Children-Affected-by-War

*L*IVING *V*ALUES:
An Educational Program

Taking Place in 64 Countries

Argentina	Hungary	Portugal
Australia	Iceland	Reunion
Austria	India	Russia
Barbados	Ireland	Singapore
Belgium	Israel	Slovakia
Bolivia	Italy	South Africa
Botswana	Jamaica	South Korea
Brazil	Japan	Spain
Canada	Jordan	Sri Lanka
Chile	Kenya	Surinam
China	Kuwait	Sweden
Colombia	Lebanon	Switzerland
Costa Rica	Malaysia	Thailand
Denmark	Mauritius	Trinidad
Ecuador	Mexico	Turkey
Egypt	Netherlands	UAE
El Salvador	New Zealand	UK
France	Nigeria	Uruguay
Germany	Peru	USA
Greece	Philippines	Zambia
Guatemala	Poland	Zimbabwe
Guyana		

Living Values:
An Educational Program

Three Core Assumptions

- Universal values teach respect and dignity for each and every person. Learning to enjoy those values promotes well-being for individuals and the larger society.

- Each student cares about values and has the capacity to positively create and learn when provided with opportunities.

- Students thrive in a values-based atmosphere in a positive, safe environment of mutual respect and care— where students are regarded as capable of learning to make socially conscious choices.

LIVING VALUES:
An Educational Program

Children are naturally curious, eager to learn,
and have many beautiful qualities.
They are creative, caring,
and can think for themselves.
In a values-based atmosphere
they bloom and thrive.

Handouts and Overhead Masters

LIVING VALUES:
An Educational Program

A Child needs . . . in relation to feelings

To feel loved.

To feel understood.

To feel respected.

To feel valued.

To feel safe.

LIVING VALUES:
An Educational Program

Emotion: Feeling Loved

Values-Based Teacher Attitudes and Actions   **Value**

Attitude: **Love**

In our classrooms, we can create an environment where children, young people, and adults can express themselves, and feel loved because of who they are—not only because of what they say, have or do.

When I enjoy children and observe the process, I can stay happy within.

Enjoying and believing in students allows them to accept and
believe in themselves.

Behaviors:
- Showing warmth, caring and kindness
- Affirming the positive qualities in each child
- Creating a healthy environment in which children can grow and develop holistically, without favoring some students over others

*L*IVING *V*ALUES:
An Educational Program

Emotion: Feeling Understood

Values-Based Teacher Attitudes and Actions **Value**

Attitude: **Love**
Each child is an individual with her or **Respect**
his own emotions and process.
Each student can learn best when her or
his emotions and level of readiness are accepted and respected.

Behaviors:

- Listening.
- Giving the space to express their feelings and ideas.
- Giving the space to accept, and process with clarity the answers
  to their needs and to situations.
- Listening openly, without expecting certain answers.
- Listen without expectations.
- Being open and flexible to students' ideas.

When not listened to, people often feel
disrespected or insignificant.

*L*iving *V*alues:
An Educational Program

Emotion: Feeling Respected

Values-Based Teacher Attitudes and Actions   **Value**

Attitude:
In the classroom, I can establish a
climate of mutual respect and understanding.   **Respect**

Behaviors:
- Listening carefully and attentively.
- Listening to what the student is really saying.
- Taking the time—recognizing the emotions.
- Establishing classroom norms with the students.
- Setting limits and being clear when students are outside the norms.
- The educator's tone of voice in the classroom is consistent with creating a values-based atmosphere. According to the situation, sometimes the tone of voice may be caring, enthusiastic, or encouraging; at other times it may be clear, firm or serious.

*L*iving *V*alues:
An Educational Program

Emotion: Feeling Valued

Values-Based Teacher Attitudes and Actions.   **Value**

Attitude: **Respect**
I believe each student can learn and   **Tolerance**
progress at many different levels.

I value each student and believe in her or his ability
to understand and learn to be peaceful and happy.

I am a facilitator of change. I have a clear
vision of the task.

Behaviors:
- Showing enthusiasm about the student and the task.
- Communicating high expectations through the belief
  in each
  student's ability to learn.
- Creating positive learning situations to help students
  understand and learn, accepting where they are.
- Present challenges and aims within their reach.
  Success increases their interest and boosts their confidence.
- Affirm positive change and actions, highlighting students'
  progress.
- The attitude, eyes and face of the educator generate
  enthusiasm and happiness through valuing each person.

*L*IVING *V*ALUES:
An Educational Program

Emotion: Feeling Safe

Values-Based Teacher Attitudes and Actions   **Value**

Attitude: **Peace**

The classroom is a place where each   **Respect**
one of us can experience dignity and being safe.

Behaviors:

- Treating mistakes as a source of information
  and a starting point for new learning.
- Asserting that no one is allowed to harm others,
  and no one will be harmed.
- Giving guidance in ways of being, how to behave,
  and what to do and not do.
- Generating understanding during discussions to
  help students make better decisions.
- Being consistent and clear about norms of behavior
  and carrying through fair consequences in a
  matter-of-fact manner.

*L*iving *V*alues:
An Educational Program

Values are the brushstrokes which give meaning to our lives. They color human reality with new ways of understanding, creating in us the passion to carry out our plans. In our quest for excellence, we overlook the easy path, the one we all know inherently. Running through our learning process is the invisible path of feelings and characteristics.

To encourage students along this path, it is necessary to provide activities that introduce quality change not only in what students "learn" but also in what they "become."

Living Values Educators' Kit

LIVING VALUES:
An Educational Program
Theoretical Model

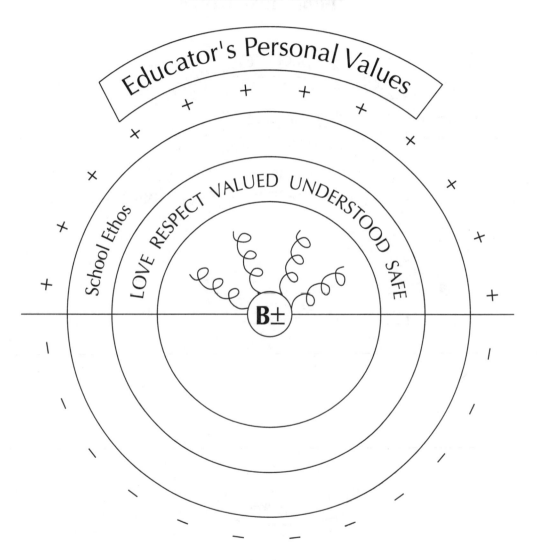

Living Values:
An Educational Program

Theoretical Model

Positive Examples:

Clear Communication
Clear Rules
Conflict Resolution Skills
Commitment to Build Success
Caring Communication
Good Staff Relations
Respectful Relationships
Homework Club
Parent Values Groups
Creativity with Drama and Arts
Listening
Teachers Model Values
Encouragement
Interesting Classes
Values Activities
Peer Mediation
Counseling

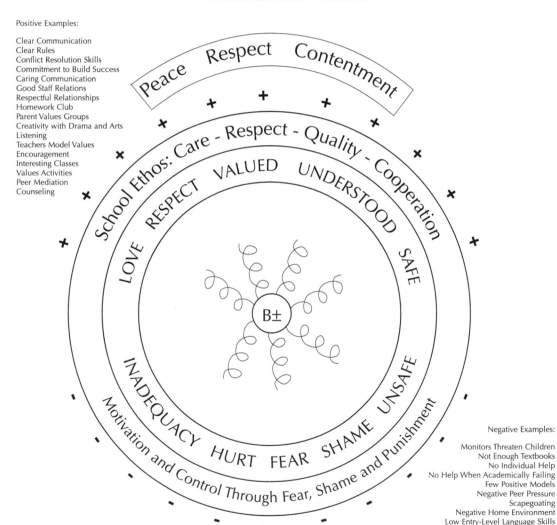

Peace   Respect   Contentment

School Ethos: Care - Respect - Quality - Cooperation

LOVE   RESPECT   VALUED   UNDERSTOOD   SAFE

B±

INADEQUACY   HURT   FEAR   SHAME   UNSAFE

Motivation and Control Through Fear, Shame and Punishment

Negative Examples:

Monitors Threaten Children
Not Enough Textbooks
No Individual Help
No Help When Academically Failing
Few Positive Models
Negative Peer Pressure
Scapegoating
Negative Home Environment
Low Entry-Level Language Skills
Shaming Punishment
Culture of Blame
Yelling

Handouts and Overhead Masters

LIVING VALUES:
An Educational Program

A Variety of Values Activities

- Reflection Points

- Imagining

- Relaxation/Focusing Exercises

- Artistic Expression

- Self-Development Activities

- Cognitive Awareness of Social Justice

- Developing Skills for Social Cohesion

These values activities are only the beginning

- Create your own.
- Emerge the values of your own culture(s).

_L_IVING _V_ALUES:
An Educational Program

Active Listening and Conflict Resolution

Blockers and Stoppers

- Accusing

- Admonishing

- Blaming

- Diminishing

- Distracting

- Giving Solutions

- Judging

- Moralizing

- Punishing

- Sympathizing

*L*IVING *V*ALUES:
An Educational Program

Conflict Resolution Steps

- Please tell us what happened.

- How did you feel when that happened?

- What would you like to stop?

- What would you like him/her to do instead?

- Can you do that?

- Can you make a firm commitment to try to behave in the way you both have agreed?

If one of them says "no," ask each student to think of something he or she would like the two to do that would solve the problem. Ask them to think of ideas until they both agree they have a good solution and can commit to trying to carry it through.

*L*IVING *V*ALUES:
An Educational Program

Conflict Resolution Steps
Ask each student: Do you want help?

To Student 1:
Please tell us what happened.

To Student 2:
Please repeat what he/she said.

To Student 2:
Please tell us what happened.

To Student 1:
Please repeat what he/she said.

To Student 1:
How did you feel when that happened?

To Student 2:
Please repeat what he/she said.

To Student 2:
How did you feel when that happened?

To Student 1:
Please repeat what he/she said.

To Student 1:
What would you like to stop?

To Student 2:
Please repeat what he/she said.

To Student 2:
What would you like to stop?

To Student 1:
Please repeat what he/she said.

To Student 1:
What would you like him to do instead?

To Student 2:
Please repeat what he/she said.

To Student 1:
What would you like her to do instead?

To Student 2:
Please repeat what he/she said.

To Student 1:
Can you do that?

To Student 2:
Can you do that?

To both: Can you make a firm commitment to try to behave in the way you both have agreed?

If one of them says "no," ask each student to think of something he or she would like the two to do that would solve the problem. Ask them to think of ideas until they both agree they have
a good solution and can commit to trying to carry it through.

Handouts and Overhead Masters

*L*iving *V*alues:
An Educational Program

Evaluation Is . . .

- the art of knowing, understanding, learning and creating.

- the process of communicating and helping students improve.

- a strategy that helps teachers plan and make practical adjustments in the classroom—for both students and teachers.

- the process of helping students emerge and develop within themselves constructive attitudes and values.

Evaluation takes into account the learning process: understanding the difficulties; the previous ideas; the attitudes; and personal factors.

*L*IVING *V*ALUES:
An Educational Program

Factors to Consider:

- Positive, constructive attitudes

- High but realistic goals

- Self-confidence and trust in the self

- Enthusiastic attitudes

- Ability to be co-operative and caring

- Ability to communicate

- Ability to accept mistakes and continue forward

$\mathcal{L}$IVING $\mathcal{V}$ALUES:
An Educational Program

Training Components

1. **Introductory Session**
   Session 1 Welcome and Opening Remarks
   Session 2: Putting the Training into Context
   Session 3: History and Overview of LVEP
   Session 4: Introductory Activities

2. **Values Awareness**
   Session 1: Our Values, Values Development in Children
   Session 2: Exploring Our Values As Teachers

3. **Creating a Values-Based Atmosphere**
   Session 1: Rekindling the Dream
   Session 1: A Tool Kit

4. **LVEP Components**

5. **Values Activities with Educators**
   First Series of Sessions: Doing the Values Activities
   Next Session: Processing the Experience, Sharing Ideas

6. **Skills to Create a Values-Based Atmosphere**
   Session 1: Acknowledgement, Encouragement and Positively
   Building Behaviors
   Session 2: Active Listening
   Session 3: Transitioning to Values-Based Discipline
   Session 4: Conflict Resolution

7. **The Process of Evaluation**

8. **Evaluation and Monitoring Forms**

9. **Using the Educator Training Guide**

10. **Adult Presentation Skills**

11. **Goals and Implementation Strategies**

12. **Closing Session**

Handouts and Overhead Masters

Adult Learning Characteristics

Research and psychologists have identified a number of characteristics that adult learners share.

- Goal oriented

- Past learning experiences

- Ingrained habits

- Actively involved

- Relate what they're learning to what they already know

- Motivated to learn when the material seems relevant

Facilitation Tips

- Listen.

- If you don't know the answer to a question, be honest and say so. Then, find out the answer and report back.

- Build rapport with participants on a one-on-one basis. Chat with them during break

- It is not necessary to "defend" the material, only to communicate it effectively.

- Recognize the importance of eye contact. As you facilitate a discussion, make eye contact with participants.

- Don't lecture or talk constantly. Ask questions or give examples to keep interest level up and to check for understanding.

- If topic is lingering too long, wrap up main points and move on.

- Never laugh at anyone—laugh with them.

- Be yourself. Be natural. Relax. Enjoy.

CITED MATERIALS

Convention on the Rights of the Child. Adopted by the General Assembly of the United Nations on November 20, 1989.

Delors, Jacques, et al. *Learning: The Treasure Within,* Report to UNESCO of the International Commission on Education for the Twenty-First Century. UNESCO Publishing, 1996. ISBN: 0-7306-9037-7

Living Values: A Guidebook. San Francisco: Brahma Kumaris, 1995.

Living Values: An Educational Initiative. *Living Values Educators' Kit,* New York: Brahma Kumaris, 1997.

North, Vanda with Buzan, Tony, *Get Ahead: Mind Map Your Way to Success.* Limited Edition Publishing: Buzan Centre Books, Bournemouth, U.K. ISBN: 1-874374-007.

Naraine, G.; Malet de Carteret, N.; Drake, C.: *Visions of a Better World.* A United Nations Peace Messenger Publication. London: Brahma Kumaris, 1993. ISBN: 0-9637396-8-9.

ABOUT THE AUTHORS

Diane G. Tillman is a licensed educational psychologist who worked in the California public school system, USA, for twenty-three years. Diane travels widely internationally, lecturing on personal development and training educators. She has worked with LVEP since its inception, and continues to develop content and training materials. She has served with the United Nations Association–USA at the local, regional and national levels.

Pilar Quera Colomina is an educator who worked in the public school system in Spain for twenty-eight years. Her experience encompasses pre-primary, primary and secondary levels of education. She was part of the initial group of twenty educators who gathered at UNICEF offices in New York to begin the Living Values Educational program. Pilar has continued to develop materials for the project, and travels widely to conduct LVEP trainings around the world.

Living Values Series

Code #8792 • Paperback • $19.95

Code #8806 • Paperback • $19.95

Living Values Activities for Young Adults

Code #8814 • Paperback • $19.95

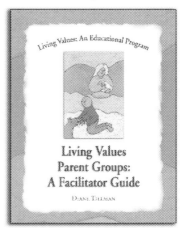

Code #8822 • Paperback • $10.95

LVEP Educator Training Guide

Code #8330 • Paperback • $12.95

To order direct: Phone **800.441.5569** • Online **www.hci-online.com**
Prices do not include shipping and handling. Your response code is **BKS**.

Growing Souls

Code #8008 • Paperback • $12.95

Code #7613 • Paperback • $12.95

Code #6099 • Paperback • $12.95

Code #6161 • Paperback • $12.95

Code #8121 • Paperback • $12.95

Code #4630 • Paperback • $12.95

Code #6374 • Paperback • $12.95

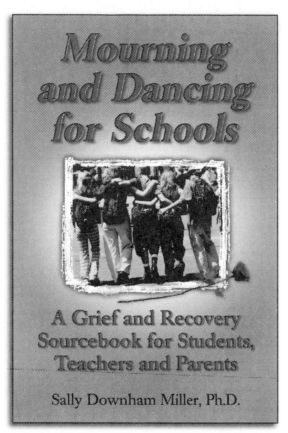

Code #7753 • Paperback • $10.95

"Grieving can be a life-long process that goes through many stages after a trauma has occurred and the headlines are gone. This book picks up where the road forks and provides a path of hope for kids and families who have experienced pain and loss."
—Montel Williams

Every school community experiences losses. Students need to be taught to acknowledge their grief. This book provides a model around this premise and shares stories of other people's losses, as well as the author's interventions with these children and their schools. It also works as a training manual and provides instructions for training a team of people to help students cope with loss.